William Winter

The Trip to England

Second Edition

William Winter

The Trip to England
Second Edition

ISBN/EAN: 9783337142582

Printed in Europe, USA, Canada, Australia, Japan

Cover: Foto ©Andreas Hilbeck / pixelio.de

More available books at **www.hansebooks.com**

THE
TRIP TO ENGLAND.

BY

WILLIAM WINTER.

Second Edition, Revised and Enlarged.

WITH ILLUSTRATIONS BY JOSEPH JEFFERSON.

BOSTON:
JAMES R. OSGOOD AND COMPANY.
1881.

Copyright 1878 and 1880,
By WILLIAM WINTER.

All Rights Reserved.

*University Press:
John Wilson and Son, Cambridge.*

✠

TO

WHITELAW REID,

WITH ESTEEM FOR HIS PUBLIC CAREER,
WITH HONOUR FOR HIS PURE CHARACTER,
AND WITH AFFECTIONATE FRIENDSHIP,

THIS MEMORIAL

OF LOVELY SCENES AND HAPPY MOMENTS

IS DEDICATED

BY

THE AUTHOR.

✠

CONTENTS.

✠

	PAGE
I. THE VOYAGE	11
II. THE BEAUTY OF ENGLAND	19
III. RAMBLES IN LONDON	30
IV. A VISIT TO WINDSOR	39
V. THE PALACE OF WESTMINSTER	48
VI. WARWICK AND KENILWORTH	57
VII. STRATFORD-ON-AVON	64
VIII. A GLIMPSE OF FRANCE	75
IX. ENGLISH HOME SUNSHINE	84
X. LONDON NOOKS AND CORNERS	89
XI. THE TOWER AND THE BYRON MEMORIAL	98
XII. WESTMINSTER ABBEY	106
XIII. THE HOME OF SHAKESPEARE	119

✠

LIST OF ILLUSTRATIONS.

HELIOTYPES, FROM SKETCHES BY JOSEPH JEFFERSON.

✠

    I. WINDSOR CASTLE.
   II. WINDSOR PARK.
  III. THE VICTORIA TOWER, AT WESTMINSTER.
  IV. THE THAMES FROM RICHMOND.
   V. THE AVENUE AT GUY'S CLIFF.
  VI. WARWICK CASTLE ON THE AVON.
 VII. THE ROAD TO STRATFORD.
VIII. DISTANT VIEW OF KENILWORTH.
  IX. ROUEN.

✠

PREFACE.

✠

THE letters that form this volume were first published in the New-York Tribune, from which journal they are now reprinted, with a few changes and additions. Their writer passed ten weeks of the summer of 1877 in England and France, where he met with a great and surprising kindness, and where he saw many beautiful and memorable things. These letters were written because he wished to commemorate — however inadequately — a delightful experience: and they are now presented in this form, at the kind request of many persons — strangers as well as friends — to whom, and to all other readers, it is hoped they may bring an hour of peaceful and pleasant reverie.

W. W.

New-York, November 16th, 1878.

✠

NOTE TO THE SECOND EDITION.

✠

THE text of this volume has been revised, for the present edition, by the correction of one or two errors, and by the improvement of a few phrases. A chapter also has been added, containing a paper on The Home of Shakespeare, written by me for Harper's Magazine, and first published in May, 1879, to record, for the American public, the dedication of the Shakespeare Memorial, at Stratford. That paper was embellished, in the Magazine, with beautiful illustrations,—equally poetical and truthful,—by Edward A. Abbey. A repetition of somewhat familiar facts was found unavoidable by the writer, but perhaps this will not be found tedious by the reader.

W. W.

Fort Hill, New Brighton, S. I.
June 21, 1880.

✠

THE TRIP TO ENGLAND.

✠

This royal throne of kings, this sceptred isle,
This earth of majesty, this seat of Mars,
This other Eden, demi-paradise,
This fortress built by nature for herself,
This precious stone set in the silver sea,
This blessèd plot, this earth, this realm, this England,
This land of such dear souls, this dear, dear land,
Dear for her reputation through the world!

SHAKESPEARE.

✠

THE TRIP TO ENGLAND.

I.

THE VOYAGE.

THE coast line recedes and disappears, and night comes down upon the ocean. Into what dangers will the great ship plunge? Through what mysterious waste of waters will she make her viewless path? The black waves roll up around her. The strong blast fills her sails and whistles through her creaking cordage. Overhead the stars shine dimly amidst the driving clouds. Mist and gloom close in the dubious prospect, and a strange sadness settles upon the heart of the voyager — who has left his home behind, and who now seeks, for the first time, the land, the homes, and the manners of the stranger. Thoughts and images of the past crowd thick upon his remembrance. The faces of absent friends rise up before him, whom, perhaps, he is destined never more to behold. He sees their smiles; he hears their voices; he fancies them by familiar hearth-stones, in the light of the evening lamps. They are very far away now; and already it seems months instead of hours since the parting moment. Vain now the pang of regret for misunderstandings, unkindness, neglect; for golden moments slighted, and gentle courtesies left undone. He is alone upon the wild sea — all the more alone because surrounded with new faces of unknown companions — and the best he can do is to seek his lonely pillow, and lie down with a prayer in his heart and on his lips. Never before did he so clearly know — never again will he so deeply feel — the uncertainty of human life and the weakness of human nature. Yet, as he notes the rush and throb of the vast ship, and the noise of the breaking waves around her, and thinks of the mighty deep beneath, and the broad and melancholy expanse that stretches away on every side, he cannot miss the impression — grand, noble, and thrilling — of human courage, skill, and power. For this ship is the centre of a splendid conflict. Man and the elements are here at war; and man makes conquest of the elements by using them as weapons against themselves. Strong and brilliant, the head-light streams over the boiling surges. Lanthorns gleam

in the tops. Dark figures keep watch upon the
prow. The officer of the night is at his post
upon the bridge. Let danger threaten howsoever it may, it cannot come unawares ; it cannot
subdue, without a tremendous struggle, the brave
minds and hardy bodies that are here arrayed to
meet it. With this thought, perhaps, the weary
voyager sinks to sleep ; and this is his first night
at sea.

There is no tediousness of solitude to him who
has within himself resources of thought and dream,
the pleasures and pains of memory, the bliss and
the torture of imagination. It is best to have few
acquaintances — or none at all — on shipboard.
Human companionship, at some times (and this
is one of them), distracts by its pettiness. The
voyager should yield himself to nature, now, and
meet his own soul face to face. The routine of
every-day life is commonplace enough, equally
upon sea and land. But the ocean is a continual
pageant, filling and soothing the mind with unspeakable peace. Never, in even the grandest
words of poetry, was the grandeur of the sea expressed. Its vastness, its freedom, its joy, and its
beauty overwhelm the mind. All things else seem
puny and momentary beside the life which by
this immense creation is unfolded and inspired.
Sometimes it shines in the sun, a wilderness of
shimmering silver. Sometimes its long waves are
black, smooth, glittering, and dangerous. Some-

times it seems instinct with a superb wrath, and its huge masses rise, and clash together, and break into crests of foam. Sometimes it is grey and quiet, as if in a sullen sleep. Sometimes the white mist broods upon it, and deepens the sense of awful mystery by which it is forever enwrapped. At night, its surging billows are furrowed with long streaks of phosphorescent fire : or, it may be, the waves roll gently, under the soft light of stars ; or all the waste is dim, save where, beneath the moon, a glorious pathway, broadening out to the far horizon, allures and points to heaven. One of the most exquisite delights of the voyage, whether by day or night, is to lie upon the deck, in some secluded spot, and look up at the tall, tapering spars as they sway with the motion of the ship, while over them the white clouds float, in ever-changing shapes, or the starry constellations drift, in their eternal march. No need now of books, or newspapers, or talk ! The eyes are fed by every object they behold. The great ship, with all her white wings spread, careening like a tiny sail-boat, dips and rises, with sinuous, stately grace. The clank of her engines — fit type of steadfast industry and purpose — goes steadily on. The song of the sailors — " Give me some time to blow the man down " — rises in cheery melody, full of audacious, light-hearted thoughtlessness, and strangely tinged with the romance of the sea. Far out toward the horizon a school of whales come sporting and spouting along. At once, out of the distant bank of cloud and mist, a little vessel springs into view, and with short, jerking movement — tilting up and down like the miniature barque upon an old Dutch clock — dances across the vista and vanishes into space. Soon a tempest bursts upon the calm ; and then, safe-housed from the fierce blast and blinding rain, the voyager exults over the stern battle of winds and waters, and the stalwart, undaunted strength with which his ship bears down the furious floods and stems the gale. By and by a quiet hour is given, when, met together with all the companions of his journey, he stands in the hushed cabin, and hears the voice of prayer and the hymn of praise ; and, in the pauses, a gentle ripple of waves against the ship, which now rocks lazily upon the quiet deep — and, ever and anon, as she dips, he can discern through her open ports the shining sea, and the wheeling and circling gulls that have come out to welcome her to the shores of the Old World.

The present writer, when first he saw the distant and dim coast of Britain, felt with a sense of forlorn loneliness, that he was a stranger; but, when last he saw that coast, he beheld it through a mist of tears, and knew that he had parted from many cherished friends, from many of the gentlest men and women upon the earth, and from a land henceforth as dear to him as his own. England is a country which to see is to love. As you draw

near to her shores you are pleased, at once, with
the air of careless finish and negligent grace
which everywhere overhangs the prospect. The
grim, wind-beaten hills of Ireland have first been
passed — hills crowned, here and there, with dark,
fierce towers that look like strongholds of ancient bandit chiefs, and cleft by dim valleys that
seem to promise endless mystery and romance,
hid in their sombre depths. Passed also is white
Queenstown, with its lovely little bay, its circle
of green hill-sides, and its valiant fort; and picturesque Fastnet, with its gaily painted tower, has
long been left behind. It is off the noble crags
of Holyhead that the voyager first observes with
what a deft skill the hand of art has here moulded
nature's luxuriance into forms of seeming chance-
born beauty; and from that hour, wherever in
rural England the footsteps of the pilgrim may
roam, he will behold nothing but gentle rustic
adornment, that has grown with the grass and
the roses — greener grass and redder roses than
ever we see in our Western World! In the
English nature a love of the beautiful is sponta-
neous; and the operation of it is as effortless as
the blowing of the summer wind. Portions of
English cities, indeed, are hard, and harsh, and
coarse enough to suit the most utilitarian taste;
yet, even in these regions of dreary monotony,
the national love of flowers will find expression,
and the people, without being aware of it, will, in

many odd little ways beautify their homes and
make their surroundings pictorial, at least to stranger eyes. There is a tone of rest and home-like
comfort even in murky Liverpool; and great magnificence is there — as well of architecture and opulent living as of enterprize and action. "Towered
cities" and "the busy hum of men," however,
are soon left behind by the wise traveller in England. A time will come for these; but in his first
sojourn there he soon discovers the two things
which are utterly to absorb him — which cannot disappoint — and which are the fulfilment of
all his dreams, and the reward of all his patience
and labour: These things are — the rustic loveliness of the land, and the charm of its always vital
and splendid antiquity. The green lanes, the
thatch-roof cottages, the meadows glorious with
wild flowers, the little churches covered with dark-green ivy, the Tudor fronts festooned with roses,
the devious foot-paths that wind across wild heaths
and long and lonesome fields, the narrow, shining
rivers, brimful to their banks, and crossed here
and there with grey and moss-grown bridges, the
stately elms, whose low-hanging branches droop
over a turf of emerald velvet, the gnarled beech-trees " that wreathe their old, fantastic roots so
high," the rooks that caw and circle in the air,
the sweet winds that blow from fragrant woods, the
sheep and the deer that rest in shady places, the
pretty children who cluster round the porches of

their cleanly, cosey homes, and peep at the wayfarer as he passes, the numerous and often brilliant birds that at times fill the air with music, the brief, light, pleasant rains that ever and anon refresh the landscape — these are some of the every-day joys of rural England ; and these are wrapped in a climate that makes life one serene ecstacy. Meantime, in rich valleys or on verdant slopes, a thousand old castles and monasteries, ruined or half in ruins, allure the pilgrim's gaze, inspire his imagination, arouse his memory, and fill his mind. The best romance of the past and the best reality of the present are his banquet now ; and nothing is wanting to the perfection of the feast. I thought that life could have but few moments of happiness in store for me like the moment — never to be forgotten ! — when, in the heart of London, on a perfect June day, I lay upon the grass in the old Green Park, and, for the first time, looked up to the towers of Westminster Abbey.

II.

THE BEAUTY OF ENGLAND.

LONDON, July 7th, 1877. — It is not strange that Englishmen should be — as certainly they are — passionate lovers of their country ; for their country is, almost beyond parallel, peaceful, gentle and beautiful. Even in this vast city, where practical life asserts itself with such prodigious force, the stranger is impressed, in every direction, with a sentiment of repose and peace. This sentiment seems to proceed in part from the antiquity of the social system here established, and in part from the affectionate nature of the English people. Here are finished towns, rural regions thoroughly cultivated and exquisitely adorned : ancient architecture, crumbling in slow decay ; and a soil so rich and pure that even in its idlest mood it lights itself up with flowers, just as the face of a sleeping child lights itself up with smiles. Here, also, are soft and kindly manners, settled principles, good laws, wise customs — wise, because rooted in the universal attributes of human nature; and, above all, here is the practice of trying to live in a happy condition, instead of trying to make a noise about it. Here, accordingly, life is soothed and hallowed with the comfortable, genial, loving spirit of home. It would, doubtless, be easily possible to come into contact here with absurd forms and pernicious abuses, to observe absurd individuals, and to trace out veins of sordid selfishness and of evil and sorrow. But the things that first and most deeply impress the fresh observer of England and English society are their potential, manifold, and abundant sources of beauty, refinement, and peace. There are, of course, grumblers. Mention has been made of a person who, even in heaven, would complain that his cloud was damp and his halo a mis-fit. We cannot have perfection; but, the man who could not be happy in England — in so far, at least, as happiness depends upon external objects and influences — could not reasonably expect to be happy anywhere.

Letters tell me that New-York is hot. The statement cannot be doubted by one who remembers what July was, last year, in that city. If this July resembles its departed brother, you are all indeed, the proper objects of pity. Here the weather is literally ───── It behaved a little shabbily during the ──── days of June; but since then it has been delightful. Summer heat is perceptible for an hour or two each day, but, to the American sense it is trivial, and it causes no discomfort. Garments that we in New-York should wear in October are quite suitable for use in the London July, and at night we sleep under blankets, and could not dispense with them. Fog has refrained; though it is understood to be lurking in the Irish Sea and the British Channel, and waiting for November, when it will drift into town and grime all the new paint on the London houses. Meantime, the sky is softly blue, and full of magnificent bronze clouds; the air is cool, and, in the environs of the city, is fragrant with the scent of new-mown hay; and the grass and trees in the parks — those copious and splendid lungs of London — are green, dewy, sweet, and beautiful.

Persons "to the manner born" were lately calling the season "backward," and they went so far as to grumble at the hawthorn, as being less brilliant than in former seasons. But, in fact, to the unfamiliar sense, this bush of odourous coral has been delicious. You know it, doubtless, as one of the sweetest beauties of rural England. It deserves its reputation. We have nothing comparable with it in northern America, unless, perhaps, it be the elder, of our wild woods; and even that, with all its fragrance, lacks equal charm of colour. They use the hawthorn, or some kindred shrub, for hedges, in this country, and hence their fields are seldom disfigured with fences. As you ride through the land, you see miles and miles of meadow, traversed by these green and blooming hedge-rows — which give the country a charm quite incommunicable in words. The green of the foliage — enriched by an uncommonly humid air, and burnished by the sun — is just now in perfection, while the flowers are out in such abundance that the whole realm is one glowing pageant. I saw the other day, near Oxford, on the crest of a hill, a single patch of at least three thousand square yards of scarlet poppies. You can imagine what a glorious dash of colour that was, in a green landscape lit by the afternoon sun. Nobody could help loving a land that woos him with such beauty.

English flowers, it must often have been noticed, are exceptional for substance and pomp. The roses, in particular — though many of them, it should be said, are of French breeds — surpass all others. It may seem an extravagance to say, but it is certainly true, that these rich, firm, brilliant flowers affect you like creatures of flesh and blood. They are, in this respect, only to be described as like nothing in the world so much as the bright lips and blushing cheeks of the handsome English women who walk among them and vie with them in health and loveliness. It is easy to perceive the source of those elements of warmth and sumptuousness which are so conspicuous in the results of English taste. This a land of flowers. Even in the busiest parts of London the people decorate their houses with them, and set the sombre, fog-grimed fronts ablaze with scarlet and gold. These are the prevalent colours (so radically such that they have become national), and, when placed against the black tint with which this climate stains the buildings, they have the advantage of a vivid contrast which much augments their splendour. All London wears "a suit of sables," variegated with a tracery of white, like lace upon a pall. In some instances the effect is splendidly pompous. There cannot be a grander artificial object in the world than the front of St. Paul's Cathedral, which is especially notable for this mysterious blending of light and shade. It is to be deplored that a climate which can thus beautify should also destroy; but there can be no doubt that the stones of England are steadily defaced by the action of the moist atmosphere. Already the delicate carvings on the Palace of Westminster are beginning to crumble. And yet, if one might judge the climate by this glittering July, England is a land of sunshine as well as of flowers. Light comes before three o'clock in the morning, and it lasts, through a dreamy and lovely "gloaming," till nearly ten o'clock at night. The morning sky is usually light blue, dappled with slate-coloured clouds. A few large stars are visible then, lingering to outface the dawn. Cool winds whisper, and presently they rouse the great, sleepy, old elms ; and then the rooks — which are the low comedians of the air, in this region — begin to grumble ; and then the sun leaps above the horizon, and we sweep into a day of golden, breezy cheerfulness and comfort, the like of which is rarely or never known in New-York, between June and October. Sometimes the whole twenty-four hours have drifted past, as if in a dream of light, and fragrance, and music. In a recent moonlight time there was scarce any darkness at all ; and more than once or twice I have lain awake all night — within a few miles of Charing Cross — listening to the twitter of small birds and the song of a nightingale, which is like the lapse and fall of silver water. It used to be difficult to understand why the London season should begin in May and last through most of the summer ; it is not difficult to understand the custom now.

The season is at its height. Parliament is in session. Both of the opera houses are open. Hyde Park is alive with riders and drivers. Theatres are alert and competitive. The clubs are thronged. The Briton is giving his serious attention to dinner. The garden party makes itself heard in the land. The excursionist is more industrious than even the Colorado beetle. Something happens every day, to interest and amuse everybody. Apart from the gay incidents of the

The Beauty of England

season, however, there is so much else to be seen in London that the pilgrim scarcely knows where to choose, and certainly is perplexed by what Dr. Johnson called "the multiplicity of agreeable consciousness." One spot, to which I have many times been drawn, and which the mention of Dr. Johnson instantly calls to mind, is the wonderously impressive place in Westminster Abbey, where that great man's ashes are buried. Side by side, under the pavement of the Abbey, within a few feet of earth, sleep Johnson, Garrick, Sheridan, Henderson, Dickens, Cumberland, and Handel. Garrick's wife is buried in the same grave with her husband. Close by, some brass letters on a little slab in the pavement disclose the last resting-place of Thomas Campbell. Not far off is the body of Macaulay; while many a stroller through the nave treads upon the grave-stone of that astonishing old man, Thomas Parr, who lived in the reigns of nine princes (1483-1635), and reached the great age of 152. All parts of Westminster Abbey impress the reverential mind. It is an experience very strange and full of awe, for instance, suddenly to find your steps upon the sepulchres of such illustrious men as Burke, Pitt, Fox, and Grattan; and you come, with a thrill of more than surprise, upon such still fresh antiquity as the grave of the hapless Anne Neville, who was the daughter of Warwick and the Queen of Richard the Third. But no single spot in the great cathedral can so enthrall the imagination as that strip of storied stone beneath which Garrick, Johnson, Sheridan, Dickens, Macaulay, and Handel sleep, side by side. This writer, when lately he visited the Abbey, found a chair upon the grave of Johnson, and sat down there to rest and muse. The letters on the stone are fast wearing away; but the memory of this sturdy champion of thought can never perish, as long as the votaries of literature love their art, and honour the valiant genius which battled — through hunger, toil, and contumely — for its dignity and renown. It was a tender and right feeling which prompted the burial of Johnson close beside Garrick. They set out together to seek their fortunes in the great city. They went through privation and trial hand in hand. Each found glory in a different way: and, although parted afterward by the currents of fame and wealth, they were never sundered in affection. It was fit they should at last find their rest together, under the most glorious roof that greets the skies of England.

Fortune gave me a good first day at the Tower of London. The sky lowered. The air was very cold. The wind blew with angry gusts. The rain fell, now and then, in a chill drizzle. The river was dark and sullen. If the spirits of the dead come back to haunt any place, they surely come back to haunt this one; and this was a day for their presence. One dark ghost seemed near, at every step — the baleful shade of the grim Duke of Gloster. The little room in which the princes are said to have been murdered, by his command, was shown, and the oratory where King Henry the Sixth is supposed to have met his bloody death, and the council chamber in which Richard — after ing, in an ambush behind the arras — denounced the wretched Hastings. This latter place is now used as an armoury; but the same ceiling covers it which echoed the bitter invective of Gloster, and the rude clamour of his soldiers, when their frightened victim was plucked forth and dragged down stairs, to be beheaded on a stick of wood in the court-yard. The Tower is a place for such deeds, and you almost wonder that they do not happen still, in its gloomy chambers. The room in which the princes were killed is particularly murderous in aspect. It is an inner room, small and dark. A barred window in one of its walls fronts a window on the other side of the passage by which you approach it. This window is but a few feet from the floor, and perhaps the murderers paused to look through it, as they went to their hellish work upon the poor children of King Edward The entrance was pointed out to a secret passage by which this apartment could be approached from the foot of the Tower. In one gloomy stone chamber the crown jewels are exhibited, in a large glass case. There is a crown here, of velvet and gold, which was made for poor Anne Boleyn.

You may pass across the court-yard and pause on the spot where this miserable woman was beheaded, and you may walk thence over the ground that her last trembling footsteps traversed, to the round tower in which, at the last, she lived. Her grave is in the chancel of a little antique church, close by. I saw the cell of Raleigh, and that direful chamber which is scrawled all over with the names and emblems of prisoners who therein suffered confinement and lingering agony, nearly always ending in death; but I saw no sadder place than Anne Boleyn's tower. It seemed in the strangest way eloquent of mute suffering. It seemed to exhale grief and to plead for love and pity. Yet — what woman ever had greater love than was lavished on her! And what woman ever trampled more royally and wickedly upon human hearts! It was to Anne Boleyn that Sir Thomas Wyatt addressed those passionate lines — so fraught with her own character as well as her lover's idolatry! — which, once read, can never be forgotten :

> "Forget not yet the tried intent
> Of such a truth as I have meant;
> My great travail so gladly spent
>   Forget not yet!

> "Forget not yet when first began
> The weary life, ye know since when;
> The suit, the service, none tell can,
>   Forget not yet!

The Beauty of England.

" Forget not yet the great assays;
  The cruel wrong, the scornful ways,
  The painful patience in delays,
      Forget not yet!

" Forget not, oh, forget not this!
  How long ago hath been, and is,
  The mind that never meant amiss,
      Forget not yet!

" Forget not then thine own approved,
  The which so long hath thee so loved.
  Whose steadfast faith yet never moved, —
      Forget not this!"

III.

RAMBLES IN LONDON.

ALL old cities get rich in association, as a matter of course, and whether they will or no; but London, by reason of its great extent, as well as its great antiquity, is richer in association than any modern place on earth. The stranger scarcely takes a step without encountering some new object of interest. The walk along the Strand and Fleet street, in particular, is continually on storied ground. Old Temple Bar still stands (July, 1877), though "tottering to its fall," and marks the boundary between the two streets. The statues of Charles the First and Charles the Second on its western front, would be remarkable anywhere, as characteristic portraits. You stand beside this arch and quite forget the passing throng, and take no heed of the tumult around, as you think of Johnson and Boswell, leaning against this wall, after midnight, in the far-off times, and waking the echoes of the Temple Garden with their frolicsome laughter. The Bar is carefully propped now, and they will nurse its age as long as they can; but it is an obstruction to travel — as much so as a wall with gates in it would be across Broadway — and it must come down. (It was removed in the summer of 1878.) They will, probably, set it up, newly built, in another place. Nothing is rashly destroyed in England. They have even left untouched a little piece of the original scaffolding built around St. Paul's; and this fragment of decaying wood may still be seen, wedged between two pilasters, high upon the side of the cathedral. The Rainbow, the Mitre, the Cheshire Cheese, Dolly's Chop-House, and the Round Table — all taverns or public-houses that were frequented by the old wits — are still extant. The Cheshire Cheese is scarcely changed from what it was when Johnson, Goldsmith, and their comrades ate beefsteak pie and drank porter there, and the Doctor " tossed and gored several persons," as it was his cheerful custom to do. The benches in that room are as uncomfortable as they well could be; mere ledges of well-worn wood, on which the visitor sits bolt upright, in difficult dignity; but there is, probably, nothing on earth that would induce the owner to alter them — and he is quite right. The conservative principle in the English mind, if it has saved some trash, has saved more treasure. At the foot of Buckingham street, a little off the Strand, — where was situated an estate of George Villiers, first Duke of Buckingham, who was assassinated in 1628, and whose tomb may be seen in Henry the Seventh's chapel, in Westminster Abbey, — still stands the slowly crumbling ruin of the old Water Gate, so often mentioned as the spot where accused traitors were embarked for the Tower. The river, in former times, flowed up to this, but the land along the margin of the Thames has been redeemed, in our day, and the magnificent Victoria and Albert Embankments now hem in the river for a long distance on both sides. The Water Gate, in fact, stands in a little park on the north bank of the Thames. Not far away is the Adelphi Terrace, where Garrick lived and died [obt. January 20th, 1779, aged sixty-three], and where, in 1822, his widow expired, at a great age. The house of Garrick is let in "chambers" now. If you walk up the Strand toward Charing Cross, you presently come near to the Church of St. Martin's-in-the-Fields, which is one of the best works of Sir Christopher Wren. The fogs have stained this building with such a deftly artistic touch that its appearance has all the charm of a lovely stereoscopic view. Nell Gwyn's name is connected with St. Martin's. She used to worship there, and she left an incessant legacy to the ringers of the bell; and at stated times, to this

day, they ring it for "poor Nelly's" sake. Her funeral occurred in this church, and was very pompous, and no less a person than Tennison (afterwards Archbishop of Canterbury) preached the funeral sermon. That prelate's dust reposes in Lambeth Church, which can be seen, across the river, from this part of Westminster. If you walk down the Strand, through Temple Bar, you presently reach the Temple; and there is no place in London where the past and the present are so strangely confronted as they are here. The venerable church, so quaint with its cone-pointed turrets, was sleeping in the sunshine when first I saw it; sparrows were twittering around its spires, and gliding in and out of the crevices in its ancient walls; while from within a strain of organ music, low and sweet, trembled forth, till the air became a benediction, and every common thought and feeling was chastened away from mind and heart. The grave of Goldsmith is close to the pathway that runs beside this church, on a terrace raised above the foundation of the building, and above the little grave-yard of the Templars, that nestles at its base. As I stood beside the resting-place of that sweet poet, it was impossible not to feel both grieved and glad -- grieved at the thought of all he suffered, and of all that the poetic nature must always suffer before it will give forth its immortal music for mankind; glad that his gentle spirit found rest at last, and that time has given him the glory he would most

have prized — the affection of all true hearts. A
grey stone. coffin-shaped, and marked with a cross,—
after the fashion of the contiguous tombs of the
Templars, — is imposed upon his grave. One surface bears the inscription, " Here lies Oliver Goldsmith;" the other presents the dates of his birth
and death. I tried to call up the scene of his burial,
when, around the open grave, on that tearful April
evening. Johnson, Burke, Reynolds, Beauclerc,
Boswell, Davies, Kelly, Palmer, and the rest of that
broken circle, may have gathered to witness

> " The duties by the lawn-robed prelate paid,
> And the last rites that dust to dust conveyed."

No place could be less romantic than Southwark
is now; but there are few places in England that
possess a greater charm for the literary pilgrim.
Shakespeare lived there, and it was there that he
managed his theatre and made his fortune. Old
London Bridge spanned the Thames, at this point,
in those days, and was the only road to the Surrey
side of the river. The theatre stood near the end
of the bridge, and was thus easy of access to the
wits and beaux of London. No trace of it now remains: but a public-house called the "Globe" —
which was its name — is standing there; and the
old church of St. Saviour's — into which Shakespeare must often have entered — still braves the
storms, and still resists the encroachments of time
and change. In Shakespeare's day there were

houses on each side of London Bridge ; and, as he walked on the bank of the Thames, he could l... across to the tower, and to Baynard Castle, which had been the residence of Richard, Duke of G...ter, and could see, uplifted high in air, the spire of Old St. Paul's. The borough of Southwark was then but thinly peopled. Many of its houses, as may be seen in an old picture of the city, were surrounded by fields or gardens; and life to its inhabitants must have been comparatively rural. Now, it is packed with buildings, gridironed with railways, crowded with people, and to the last degree resonant and feverish with action and effort. Life swarms, traffic bustles, and travel thunders, all round the cradle of the British drama. The old church of St. Saviour's alone preserves the sacred memory of the past. I made a pilgrimage to this shrine, in the company of one of the kindliest humorists in England. We took boat at Westminster Bridge, and landed close by the church in Southwark, and we were so fortunate as to get permission to enter the church without a gu de. The oldest part of it is the Lady Chapel — a wing which, in English cathedrals, is placed behind the choir. Through this we strolled, alone and in silence. Every footstep there falls upon a grave. The pavement is one mass of grave-stones ; and through the lofty, stained windows of the chapel a solemn light pours in upon the sculptured names of men and women who have long been dust. In one corner is an ancient stone coffin — a relic of the Roman days of Britain. This is the room in which Stephen Gardiner — Bishop of Winchester, in the days of cruel Queen Mary — held his ecclesiastical court, and condemned many a dissentient devotee to the rack and the faggot: in this very room he had himself been put to trial, in his hour of misfortune. Both Mary and Elizabeth must often have entered this chapel. But it is in the choir, hard by, that the pilgrim pauses with most of reverence; for here, not far from the altar, he stands upon the graves of Edmund Shakespeare, John Fletcher, and Phillip Massinger. They rest almost side by side, and only their names and the dates of their death are cut in the tablets that mark their sepulchres. Edmund Shakespeare, the younger brother of William, was an actor in his company, and died in 1607, aged twenty-seven. The great poet must have stood at this grave, and suffered and wept here; and somehow the lover of Shakespeare comes very near to the heart of the master, when he stands in this place. Massinger was buried there, March 18, 1638, — the parish register recording him as "a stranger." Fletcher — of the Beaumont and Fletcher brotherhood — was buried there, in 1625: Beaumont's grave is in the Abbey. The dust of Henslowe, the manager, also rests beneath the pavement of St. Saviour's. In the north transept of the church is the tomb of John Gower, the old poet — whose effigy, carved and painted, reclines upon it, and is not pleasant to behold. A formal, uncomely, severe aspect he must have had, if he resembled this image. The tomb has been moved from the spot where it first stood — a proceeding made necessary by a fire that destroyed part of the old church. It is said that Gower caused this tomb to be erected during his life-time, so that it might be in readiness to receive his bones. The bones are lost, but the memorial remains — sacred to the memory of the father of English song. This tomb was restored by the Duke of Sutherland, in 1830. It is enclosed by a little fence made of iron spears, painted brown and gilded at their points. I went into the new part of the church, and, quite alone, knelt in one of the pews, and long remained there, overcome with thoughts of the past, and of the transient, momentary nature of this our earthly life and the shadows that we pursue.

One object of merriment attracts a passing glance in Southwark Church. There is a tomb in a corner of it, that commemorates an ancient maker of patent medicine — an elaborate structure, with the deceased cut in effigy, and with a long and sonorous epitaph on the pedestal. These are two of the lines:

> "His virtues and his Pills are so well known,
> That envy can't confine them under stone."

Shakespeare once lived in Clink street, in the borough of Southwark. Goldsmith practised medicine there, for a while. Chaucer came there, with his Canterbury Pilgrims, and stopped at the Tabard Inn. It must have been a romantic region, in the old times : but it bears now the same relation to London that Brooklyn bears to New-York — except that it is more populous, active, and noisy.

IV.

A VISIT TO WINDSOR.

IF the beauty of England were merely superficial it would produce a merely superficial
effect. It would cause a passing pleasure, and
be forgotten. It certainly would not — as
fact it does — inspire a deep, joyous, serene
contentment, and linger in the mind,
and beneficent remembrance. The con-
and lasting potency of it resides not
alone loveliness of expression, but in loveliness
er. Having first greatly blessed the
Islands with the of
climate, soil, and p nature has
out their development and
a consequence of the spirit of
ts. The

repose of the English landscape spring, in a considerable measure, from the imaginative taste and the affectionate gentleness of the English people. The state of the country, like its social constitution, flows from principles within (which are constantly suggested), and it steadily comforts and nourishes the mind with a sense of kindly feeling, moral rectitude, solidity, and permanence. Thus in the peculiar beauty of England the ideal is made the actual — is expressed in things more than in words; and in things by which words are transcended. Milton's "L'Allegro," fine as it is, is not so fine as the scenery — the crystallized, embodied poetry — out of which it arose. All the delicious rural verse that has been written in England is only the excess and superflux of her own poetic opulence; it has rippled from the hearts of her poets just as the fragrance floats away from her hawthorn hedges. At every step of his progress the pilgrim through English scenes is impressed with this sovereign excellence of the accomplished fact, as contrasted with any words that can be said in its celebration.

Among representative scenes which are eloquent with this instructive meaning, — scenes easily and pleasurably accessible to the traveller, in what Dickens expressively called "the green, English summer weather," — is the region of Windsor. The chief features of it have often been described; the charm that it exercises can only be suggested.

A Visit to Windsor.

To see Windsor, moreover, is to comprehend, as at a glance, the old feudal system, and to feel, in a profound and special way, the pomp of English character and history. More than this: It is to rise to that ennobling exaltation which always accompanies broad, retrospective contemplation of the current of human affairs. In this quaint, decorous town — nestled at the base of that mighty and magnificent castle which has been the home of princes for more than five hundred years — the imaginative mind wanders over vast tracts of the past, and beholds, as in a mirror, the pageants of chivalry, the coronations of kings, the strifes of sects, the battles of armies, the schemes of statesmen, the decay of transient systems, the growth of a rational civilization, and the everlasting march of thought. Every prospect of the region intensifies this sentiment of contemplative grandeur. As you look from the castle walls your gaze takes in miles and miles of blooming country, sprinkled over with little hamlets, wherein the utmost stateliness of learning and rank is gracefully commingled with all that is lovely and soothing in rural life. Not far away rise the "antique towers" of Eton —

> " Where grateful Science still adores
> Her Henry's holy shade."

It was in Windsor Castle that her Henry was born; and there he often held his court; and it is in St. George's Chapel that his relics repose. In the dim distance stands the church of Stoke-Pogis, about which Gray was wont to wander,

"Beneath those rugged elms, that yew-tree's shade."

You recognize now a deeper significance than ever before in the "solemn stillness" of the incomparable Elegy. The luminous twilight mood of that immortal poem — its pensive reverie and solemn passion — is inherent in the scene; and you feel that it was there, and there only, that the genius of its exceptional author — austerely gentle and severely pure, and thus in perfect harmony with its surroundings — could have been moved to that sublime outburst of inspiration and eloquence. Near at hand, in the midst of your reverie, the mellow organ sounds from the chapel of St. George, where, under "fretted vault" and over "long-drawn aisle," depend the ghostly, mouldering banners of ancient knights — as still as the bones of the dead-and-gone monarchs that crumble in the crypt below. In this church are many of the old kings and nobles of England. The handsome and gallant Edward the Fourth here found his grave; and near it is that of the accomplished Hastings — his faithful friend, to the last and after. Here lies the dust of the stalwart, impetuous, and savage Henry the Eighth, and here the ill-starred and hapless Queen Caroline: and here, at midnight, by the light of torches, they laid beneath the pavement the mangled body of Charles the First. As you stand on Windsor ramparts, pondering thus upon the storied past and the evanescence of "all that beauty, all that wealth e'er gave," your eyes rest dreamily on green fields far below, through which, under tall elms, the brimming and sparkling river flows on without a sound, and in which a few figures, dwarfed by distance, flit here and there, in seeming aimless idleness; while, warned homeward by impending sunset, the chattering birds circle and float around the lofty towers of the castle; and delicate perfumes of seringa and jasmine are wafted up from dusky, unknown depths at the base of its ivied steep. At such an hour I stood on those ramparts, and saw the shy villages and rich meadows of fertile Berkshire, all red and golden with sunset light; and at such an hour I stood in the lonely cloisters of St. George's Chapel, and heard the distant organ sob, and saw the sunlight fade up the grey walls, and felt and knew the sanctity of silence. Age and death have made this church illustrious; but the spot itself has its own innate charm of mystical repose.

> "No use of lanthorns; and in one place lay
> Feathers and dust to-day and yesterday."

The drive from the front of Windsor Castle is through a broad and stately avenue, three miles in length, straight as an arrow and level as a standing pool; and this white highway through the green and fragrant sod is sumptuously embowered, from end to end, with double rows of magnificent old elms. The Windsor avenue, like the splendid chestnut grove at Bushy Park, long famous among the pageants of rural England, has often been described. It is after leaving this that the rambler comes upon the rarer beauties of Windsor Park and Forest. From the far end of the avenue — where, in a superb position, the equestrian statue of King George rises on its massive pedestal of natural rock, — the road winds away, through shaded dell and verdant glade, past great gnarled beeches and under boughs of elm, and yew, and oak, till its silver thread is lost in the distant woods. At intervals a branching path-way strays off to some secluded lodge, half hidden in foliage — the property of the Crown, and the rustic residence of a scion of the royal race. In one of these retreats dwelt poor old George the Third, in the days of his mental darkness; and the memory of the agonizing king seems still to cast a shadow on the mysterious and melancholy house. They show you, under glass, in one of the lodge gardens, an enormous grape-vine, owned by the Queen — a vine which, from its single stalwart trunk, spreads its teeming branches, laterally, at least two hundred feet in each direction. So come use and thrift, hand in hand with romance! Many an aged oak is passed, in your path — round which, "at still midnight," Herne the Hunter might still take his ghostly prowl, shaking his chain "in a most hideous and dreadful manner." The wreck of the veritable Herne's Oak, it is said, was rooted out, together with other ancient and decayed trees, in the time of George the Third, and in somewhat too literal fulfilment of his Majesty's misinterpreted command. This great park is fourteen miles in circumference, and contains nearly four thousand acres ; and many of the youngest trees that adorn it are more than one hundred and fifty years old. Far in its heart you stroll by Virginia Water — an artificial lake, but faultless in its quiet beauty — and perceive it so deep and so breezy that a full-rigged ship-of-war, with heavy armament, can navigate its wind-swept, curling billows. In the dim groves that fringe its margin are many nests wherein pheasants are bred, to fall by the royal shot and to supply the royal tables : these you may contemplate, but not approach. At a point in your walk, sequestered and lonely, they have set up and skilfully disposed the fragments of a genuine ruined temple, brought from the remote East — relic, perchance, of "Tadmor's marble waste," and certainly a most solemn memorial of the morning twilight of time. Broken arch, storm-stained pillar, and shattered column are here shrouded with moss and ivy : and should you chance to see them as the evening shadows deepen and the evening wind sighs mournfully in the grass, your fancy will not fail to drink in the perfect illusion that one of the stateliest structures of antiquity has slowly crumbled where now its fragments remain.

Quaint is a descriptive epithet that has been much abused; but it may, with absolute propriety, be applied to Windsor. The devious little streets there visible, and the carved and timber-crossed buildings, often of great age, are uncommonly rich in the expressiveness of imaginative character. The emotions and the fancy, equally with the sense of necessity and the instinct of use, have exercised their influence and uttered their spirit in the shaping and adornment of the town. While it constantly feeds the eye — with that pleasing irregularity of lines and forms which is so delicious and refreshing — it quite as constantly nurtures the sense of romance which ought to play so large a part in all our lives, redeeming us from the tyranny of the commonplace and intensifying all the high feelings and noble aspirations that are possible to human nature. England contains many places like Windsor; some that blend, in even richer amplitude, the elements of quaintness, loveliness, and magnificence. The meaning of them all, as it seemed to me, is the same: that romance, beauty, and gentleness are not effete, but forever vital; that their forces are within our

own souls, and ready and eager to find their way
into all our thoughts, actions, and circumstances,
and to brighten for every one of us the face of
every day; that they ought neither to be relegated
to the distant and the past, nor kept for our books
and day-dreams alone; but — in a calmer and
higher mood than is usual in this age of universal
mediocrity, critical scepticism, and miscellaneous
tumult — should be permitted to flow out into our
architecture, adornments, and customs, to hallow
and preserve our antiquities, to soften our manners,
to give us tranquillity, patience, and tolerance, to
make our country loveable for our own hearts, and
so to enable us to bequeath it, sure of love and
reverence, to succeeding ages.

V.

THE PALACE OF WESTMINSTER.

THE American who, having been a careful and interested reader of English history, visits London for the first time, naturally expects to find the ancient city in a state of mild decay; and he is, consequently, a little startled at first, upon realizing that the Present is quite as vital as ever the Past was, and that London antiquity is, in fact, swathed in the robes of every-day action, and very much alive. When, for example, you enter Westminster Hall — "the great hall of William Rufus" — you are beneath one of the most glorious canopies in the world — one which was built by Richard the Second, whose grave, chosen by himself, is in the Abbey, just across the street

from where you stand. But this old hall is now only a vestibule to the Palace of Westminster. The Lords and the Commons of England, on their way to the Houses of Parliament, pass every day over the spot on which Charles the First was tried and executed, and on which occurred the trial of Warren Hastings. It is a mere thoroughfare glorious though it be, alike in structure and historic renown. The Palace Yard, near by, was the scene of the execution of Sir Walter Raleigh; but all that now marks the spot is a rank of cabs and a shelter for cab-drivers. In Bishopsgate street — where Shakespeare once lived — you may find Crosby House; the same to which, in Shakespeare's tragedy, the Duke of Gloster requests the retirement of Lady Anne. It is a restaurant now; and you may enjoy a capital chop and excellent beer, in the veritable throne-room of Richard the Third. The house of Cardinal Wolsey, in Fleet street is now a shop. Milton once lived in Golden Lane; and Golden Lane was a sweet and quiet spot. It is a slum now, dingy and dismal, and the visitor is glad to get out of it. To-day makes use of yesterday, all the world over. It is not in London, certainly, that you find much of anything — except old churches — mouldering in silence, solitude, and neglect.

Those who see every day, during the Parliamentary session, the mace that is borne through the lobby of the House of Commons, although they are obliged, on every occasion, to remove their hats as it passes, do not, probably, view that symbol with much interest. Yet it is the same mace that Oliver Cromwell insulted, when he dissolved the Parliament, and cried out "Take away that bauble!" I saw it one day, on its passage to the table of the Commons, and was glad to remove the hat of respect to what it signifies — the power and majesty of the free people of England. The Speaker of the House was walking behind it, very grand in his wig and gown, and the members trooped in at his heels, to secure their places by being present at the opening prayer. A little later I was provided with a seat, in a dim corner, in that august assemblage of British Senators, and could observe at ease their management of the public business. The Speaker was on his throne; the mace was on its table; the hats of the Commons were on their heads; and over this singular, animated, every-day, and yet impressive scene, the waning light of a summer afternoon poured softly down, through the high, stained, and pictured windows of one of the most symmetrical halls in the world. It did not happen to be a day of excitement. The Irish members had not then begun to impede the transaction of business, for the sake of drawing attention to the everlasting wrongs of Ireland. Yet it was a lively day. Curiosity on the part of the Opposition, and a respectful dubiousness on the part of Her Majesty's representatives, were the prevailing conditions. I thought I had never before heard so many questions asked — outside of the French grammar — and asked to so little purpose. Everybody wanted to know, and nobody wanted to tell. Each inquirer took off his hat when he rose to ask, and put it on again, when he sat down to be answered. Each governmental sphinx bared his brow when he emerged to divulge, and covered it again when he subsided without divulging. The respect of all these interlocutors for each other steadily remained, however, of the most deferential and considerate description; so that — without discourtesy — it was impossible not to think of Byron's "mildest mannered man that ever scuttled ship or cut a throat." Underneath this velvety, purring, conventional manner the observer could readily discern the fires of passion, prejudice, and strong antagonism. They make no parade in the House of Commons. They attend to their business. And upon every topic that is brought before their notice they have definite ideas, strong convictions, and settled purposes. The topic of Army Estimates, upon the occasion to which I refer, seemed especially to arouse their ardour. Discussion of this was continually diversified by cries of "O!" and of "Hear!" and of "Order!" and sometimes these cries smacked more of derision than of compliment. Many persons spoke, but no person spoke well. An off-hand, matter-of-fact, shambling method of speech would seem to be the fashion, in the British

House of Commons. I remembered the anecdote that De Quincey tells, about Sheridan and the young member who quoted Greek. It was easy to perceive how completely out of place the sophomore orator would be, in that assemblage. Britons like better to make speeches than to hear them, and they never will be slaves to oratory. The moment a certain windy gentleman got the floor, and began to read a manuscript respecting the Indian Government, as many as forty Commons arose and noisily walked out of the House. Your pilgrim likewise hailed the moment of his deliverance, and was glad to escape to the open air.

Books have been written to describe the Palace of Westminster: but it is observable that this structure, however much its magnificence deserves commemorative applause, is deficient, as yet, in the charm which resides in association. The old Palace of St. James, with its low, dusky walls, its round towers, and its fretted battlements, is more impressive, because history has freighted it with meaning, and time has made it beautiful. But the Palace of Westminster is a splendid structure. It covers eight acres of ground, on the bank of the Thames; it contains eleven quadrangles and five hundred rooms; and, when its niches for statuary have all been filled, it will contain two hundred and twenty-six statues. The monuments in St. Stephen's Hall—into which you pass from Westminster Hall, which has been incorporated into the Palace,

The Palace of Westminster

and is its only ancient, and therefore its most interesting, feature — indicate, very eloquently, what a superb art-gallery this will one day become. The statues are the images of Selden, Hampden, Falkland, Clarendon, Somers, Walpole, Chatham, Mansfield, Burke, Fox, Pitt, and Grattan. Those of Mansfield and Grattan present, perhaps, the most of character and power, making you feel that they are indubitably accurate portraits, and drawing you by the charm of personality. There are statues, also, in Westminster Hall, commemorative of the Georges, William and Mary, and Anne; but it is not of these you think, nor of any local and everyday object, when you stand beneath the wonderful roof of Richard the Second. Nearly eight hundred years " their cloudy wings expand " above this fabric, and copiously shed upon it the fragrance of old renown. Richard the Second was deposed there: Cromwell was there installed Lord Protector of England; John Fisher, Sir Thomas More, and Strafford were there condemned; and it was there that the possible, if not usual, devotion of woman's heart was so touchingly displayed, by her

> "Whose faith drew strength from death,
> And prayed her Russell up to God."

No one can realize, without personal experience, the number and variety of pleasures accessible to the resident of London. These may not be piquant to him who has them always within his reach. I met with several residents of the British Capital who had always intended to visit the Tower, but had never done so. But to the stranger they possess a constant and keen fascination. The Derby this year [1877], was thought to be, comparatively, a tame race; but I know of one spectator who saw it from the top of the Grand Stand and thought that the scene it presented was wonderfully brilliant. The sky had been overcast with dull clouds till the moment when the race was won: but, just as Archer, rising in his saddle, lifted his horse forward and gained the goal alone, the sun burst forth, and shed upon the Downs a sheen of gold, and lit up all the distant hills, and all the far-stretching roads that wind away from the region of Epsom like threads of silver through the green. Carrier-pigeons were instantly launched off to London, with the news of the victory of Silvio. There was one winner on the Grand Stand who had laid bets on Silvio, for no other reason than because this horse bore the prettiest name in the list. The Derby, like Christmas, comes but once a year; but other allurements are almost perennial. Greenwich, for instance, with its delicious white-bait dinner, invites the epicure during the best part of the London season. The favourite tavern is the Trafalgar — in which each room is named after some magnate of the old British Navy; and Nelson, Hardy, and Rodney are household words. Another cheery place of resort is The Ship. The Hospitals are at Greenwich,

The Palace of Westminster.

that Dr. Johnson thought to be too fine for a charity; and back of these — which are ordinary now, in comparison with modern structures erected for a kindred purpose — stands the famous Observatory which keeps time for Europe. This place is hallowed, also, by the grave of Wolfe — to whom, however there is a monument in Westminster Abbey. Greenwich sets one thinking of Queen Elizabeth, who was born there, who often held her court there, and who often sailed thence, in her barge, up the river, to Richmond — her favourite retreat, and the scene of her last days and her wretched death. Few spots can compare with Richmond, in brilliancy of landscape. This place — the Shene of old times — was long a royal residence. The woods and meadows that you see from the terrace of the Star and Garter Tavern — spread out on a rolling plain as far as the eye can reach — sparkle like emeralds; and the Thames, dotted with little toy-like boats, propelled by the oars of coquettishly apparelled rowers, shines with all the deep lustre of the black eyes of Spain. Pope's lovely home is here, in the village of Twickenham; and not far away glimmers forth to view the "pale shrine" of the poet Thomson — whose dust is in Richmond Church. As I drove through the vast and sweetly sylvan Park of Richmond, in the late afternoon of a breezy summer day, and heard the whispering of the great elms, and saw the gentle, trustful deer couched at ease, in the golden glades, I heard all the while, in the quiet chambers of thought, the tender lament of Collins — which is now a prophecy fulfilled:

> " Remembrance oft shall haunt the shore,
>   When Thames in summer wreaths is drest;
> And oft suspend the dashing oar,
>   To bid his gentle spirit rest."

VI.

WARWICK AND KENILWORTH.

ALL the way from London to Warwick it rained; not heavily but with a gentle fall. The grey clouds hung low over the landscape, and softly darkened it: so that meadows of scarlet and emerald, the shining foliage of elms, grey turret, nestled cottage, and limpid river were as mysterious and evanescent as pictures seen in dreams. At Warwick the rain had fallen and ceased, and the walk from the station to the inn was on a road — or on a foot-path by the road-side — still hard and damp with the water it had absorbed. A fresh wind blew from the fields, sweet with the rain and fragrant with the odour of leaves and flowers. The streets of the ancient town — entered through an old Norman arch — were deserted and silent. It was Sunday when I first came to the country of Shakespeare ; and over all the region there brooded a sacred stillness peculiar to the time and harmonious beyond utterance with the sanctity of the place. As I strive, after many days, to call back and to fix in words the impressions of that sublime experience, the same awe falls upon me now which fell upon me then. Nothing else upon earth — no natural scene, no relic of the past, no pageantry of the present — can vie with the shrine of Shakespeare, in power to impress, to humble, and to exalt the devout spirit that has been nurtured at the fountain of his transcendent genius.

A fortunate way to approach Stratford-on-Avon is by Warwick and Kenilworth. These places are not on a direct line of travel ; but the scenes and associations which they successively present are such as assume a symmetrical order, increase in interest, and grow to a delightful culmination. Objects which Shakespeare himself must have seen are still visible there ; and, little by little, in contact with these, the pilgrim through this haunted region is mentally saturated with that atmosphere of serenity and romance in which the youth of Shakespeare was passed, and by which his works and his memory are embalmed. No one should come abruptly upon the Poet's Home. The mind needs to be prepared for the impression that

awaits it; and in this gradual approach it
preparation, both suitable and delicious. T
luxuriance of the country — its fertile fields, its
brilliant foliage, its myriads of wild flowers, its
pomp of colour and of physical vigour and bloom,
do not fail to announce, to every mind — howsoever
— that this is a fit place for the birth
and nurture of a great man. But this is not all.
As you stroll in the quaint streets of Warwick, as
you drive to Kenilworth, as you muse in that
poetic ruin, as you pause in the old grave-yard in
the valley below, as you pass beneath the crumbling
arch of the ancient Priory, at every step of
the way you are haunted by a vague sense of
some impending grandeur; you are aware of a
presence that fills and sanctifies the scene. The
emotion that is thus inspired is very glorious;
never to be elsewhere felt; and never to be forgotten.

The cyclopædias and the guide-books dilate,
with much particularity and characteristic eloquence,
upon Warwick Castle and other great
features of Warwickshire; and an off-hand sketch
cannot aspire, and should not attempt, to emulate
those authentic chronicles. The attribute which
all such records omit is the atmosphere; and this,
perhaps, is rather to be indicated than described.
The prevailing quality of it is a certain high and
sweet solemnity — a feeling kindred with the placid,
happy melancholy that steals over the mind.

when, on a sombre afternoon in autumn, you stand in the church-yard, and listen, amidst rustling branches and sighing grass, to the low music of distant organ and chaunting choir. Peace, haunted by romance, dwells here in reverie. The great tower of Warwick, based in silver Avon and pictured in its slumbering waters, seems musing upon the centuries over which it has watched, and full of unspeakable knowledge and thought. The dark and massive gate-ways of the town and the timber-crossed fronts of its antique houses live on in the same strange dream and perfect repose; and all along the drive to Kenilworth are equal images of rest — of a rest in which there is nothing supine or sluggish, no element of death or decay, but in which passion, imagination, beauty, and sorrow, seized at their topmost poise, seem crystallized in eternal calm. What opulence of splendid life is vital forever in Kenilworth's crumbling ruin, there are no words to say. What pomp of royal banners! what dignity of radiant cavaliers! what loveliness of stately and exquisite ladies! what magnificence of banquets! what wealth of pageantry! what lustre of illumination! The same perfect music that the old poet Gascoigne heard there, three hundred years ago, is still sounding on, to-day. The proud and cruel Leicester still walks in his vaulted hall. The imperious face of the Virgin Queen still from her dais looks down on pluméd courtiers and jeweled dames; and still the moonlight, streaming through the turret-window, falls on the white bosom and the great, startled, black eyes of Amy Robsart, waiting for her lover. The gaze of the pilgrim, indeed, rests only upon old, grey, broken walls, overgrown with green moss and ivy, and pierced by irregular casements through which the sun shines, and the winds blow, and the rains drive, and the birds fly, amidst utter desolation. But silence and ruin are here alike eloquent and awful; and, much as the place impresses you by what remains, it impresses you far more by what has vanished. Ambition, love, pleasure, power, misery, tragedy — these are gone; and being gone they are immortal. I plucked, in the garden of Kenilworth, one of the most brilliant red roses that ever grew; and, as I pressed it to my lips, I seemed to touch the lips of that superb, bewildering beauty who outweighed England's crown, and whose spirit is the everlasting genius of the place.

There is a crescent of thatch-roofed cottages close by the ruins of the old castle, in which contentment seems to have made her home. The ivy embowers them. The roses cluster around their little windows. The greensward slopes away, in front, from the big, flat stones that are embedded in the grassy sod before their doors. Down in the valley, hard by, your steps stray through an ancient grave-yard — in which modern hands have built a tiny church, with tower, and clock, and bell

— and past the remains of a Priory, long since destroyed. At many another point, on the roads betwixt Warwick and Kenilworth and Stratford, I came upon such nests of cosey, rustic quiet and seeming happiness. They build their country houses low, in England, so that the trees overhang them, and the cool, friendly, flower-gemmed earth — parent, and stay, and bourne of mortal life! — is tenderly taken into their companionship. Here, at Kenilworth, as elsewhere, at such places as Richmond, Maidenhead, Cookham, and the region round about Windsor, I saw many a sweet nook where tired life might well be content to lay down its burden and enter into its rest. In all true love of country — a passion which seems to be more deeply felt in England than anywhere else upon the globe — there is love for the literal soil itself: and that sentiment in the human heart is equally natural and pious which inspires and perpetuates man's desire that where he found his cradle he may also find his grave.

Under a cloudy sky, and through a landscape still wet and shining with recent rains, the drive to Stratford was a pleasure so exquisite that at last it became a pain. Just as the carriage reached the junction of the Warwick and Snitterfield roads, a ray of sunshine, streaming through a rift in the clouds, fell upon the neighbouring hill-side, scarlet with poppies, and lit the scene as with the glory of a celestial benediction. This sunburst, neither growing larger nor coming nearer, followed all the way to Stratford; and there, on a sudden, the clouds were lifted and dispersed, and "fair daylight" flooded the whole green country-side. The afternoon sun was still high in heaven when I alighted at the Red Horse Inn, and entered the little parlour of Washington Irving. They keep the room very much as it was when he left it; for they are proud of his gentle genius and grateful for his commemorative words. In a corner stands the small, old-fashioned hair-cloth arm-chair, in which he sat, on that night of memory and of musing which he has described in the "Sketch Book." A brass plate is affixed to it, bearing his name: and the visitor observes, in token of its age and service, that the hair-cloth of its seat is considerably worn and frayed. Every American pilgrim to Stratford sits in this chair; and looks with tender interest on the old fire-place; and reads the memorials of Irving that are hung upon the walls: and it is no small comfort there to reflect that our own illustrious countryman — whose name will be remembered with honour, as long as true literature is prized among men — was the first, in modern days, to discover the beauties and to interpret the poetry of the birth-place of Shakespeare.

VII.

STRATFORD-ON-AVON.

ONCE again, as it did on that delicious summer afternoon which is forever memorable in my life, the golden glory of the westering sun burns on the grey spire of Stratford Church, and on the ancient grave-yard below, — wherein the mossy stones lean this way and that, in sweet and orderly confusion, — and on the peaceful avenue of limes, and on the burnished water of silver Avon. The tall, arched, many-coloured windows of the church glint in the evening light. A cool and fragrant wind is stirring the branches and the grass. The small birds, calling to their mates, or sporting in the wanton pleasure of their airy life, are circling over the church roof, or

hiding in little crevices of its ⸺⸺. On the
⸺⸺ meadows across the river stretch away the
long and level shadows of the pompous elms.
Here and there, upon the river's brink, are pairs of
what seem lovers, strolling by the reedy marge,
or sitting upon the low tombs, in the Sabbath
quiet. As the sun sinks and the dusk deepens,
two figures of infirm old women, clad in black,
pass with slow and feeble steps through the
avenue of limes, and vanish around an angle of
the church — which now stands all in shadow;
and no sound is heard but the faint rustling of the
leaves.

Once again, as on that sacred night, the streets
of Stratford are deserted and silent under the
star-lit sky, and I am standing, in the dim darkness, at the door of the cottage in which Shakespeare was born. It is empty, dark, and still;
and in all the neighbourhood there is no stir nor
sign of life; but the quaint casements and gables
of this haunted house, its antique porch, and the
great timbers that cross its front are luminous
as with a light of their own, so that I see them
with perfect distinctness. I stand there a long
time, and I know that I am to remember these
sights forever, as I see them now. After a
while, with lingering reluctance, I turn away
from this marvellous spot, and, presently passing
through a little, winding lane, I walk in the High
street of the town, and mark, at the end of

the prospect, the illuminated clock in the tower of the chapel of the Holy Cross. A few chance-directed steps bring me to what was New Place once, where Shakespeare died; and there again I pause, and long remain in meditation, gazing into the inclosed garden, where, under frames of glass, are certain strange fragments of lime and stone. These — which I do not then know — are the remains of the foundation of Shakespeare's house. The night wanes; and still I walk in Stratford streets; and by and by I am standing on the bridge that spans the Avon, and looking down at the thick-clustering stars reflected in its black and silent stream. At last, under the roof of the Red Horse, I sink into a troubled slumber, from which very soon a strain of celestial music — strong, sweet, jubilant, and splendid — awakens me in an instant, and I start up in my bed — to find that all around me is still as death; and then, drowsily, far-off, the bell strikes three, in its weird and lonesome tower.

Every pilgrim to Stratford knows beforehand, in a general way, what he will there behold. Copious and frequent description of its Shakespearean associations have made the place familiar to all the world. Yet these Shakespearean associations keep a perennial freshness, and are equally a surprise to the sight and a wonder to the soul. Though three centuries old, they are not yet stricken with age or decay. The house in Henley street, in which, according to accepted tradition, Shakespeare was born, has been from time to time repaired; and so it has been kept sound, without having been materially changed from what it was in Shakespeare's youth. The kind old ladies who now take care of it, and, with so much pride and courtesy, show it to the visitor, called my attention to a bit of the ceiling of the upper chamber — the alleged room of Shakespeare's birth — which had begun to sag, and had been skilfully mended, with little laths. It is in this room that the numerous autographs are scrawled all over the ceiling and walls. One side of the chimney-piece here is called "The Actor's Pillar," so thickly is it covered with the names of actors ; Edmund Kean's signature being among them, and still clearly legible. On one of the window-panes, cut with a diamond, is the name of "W. Scott"; and all the panes are scratched with signatures — making you think of Douglas Jerrold's remark on bad Shakespearean commentators, that they resemble persons who write on glass with diamonds, and obscure the light with a multitude of scratches. The floor of this room, uncarpeted, and almost snow-white with much washing, seems still as hard as iron ; yet its boards have been hollowed by wear, and the heads of the old nails, that fasten it down, gleam like polished silver. You can sit in an antique chair, in a corner of this room, if you like, and think unutterable things. There is, certainly, no word that can even remotely suggest the feeling with which you are there overwhelmed. You can sit, also, in the room below, in the very seat, in the corner of the wide fire-place, that Shakespeare himself must often have occupied. They keep but a few sticks of furniture in any part of the cottage. One room is devoted to Shakespearean curiosities — or relics — more or less authentic; one of which is a school-boy's form or desk, that was obtained from the old grammar school in High street, now modern in its appointments, in which Shakespeare was once a pupil. At the back of the cottage, now isolated from all contiguous structures, is a pleasant garden, and at one side is a cosey, luxurious little cabin — the home of order and of pious decorum — for the ladies who are custodians of the Shakespeare House. If you are a favoured visitor, you may receive from this garden, at parting, all the flowers, prettily affixed to a sheet of purple-edged paper, that poor *Ophelia* names, in the scene of her madness. "There's rosemary, that's for remembrance: and there is pansies, that's for thoughts: there's fennel for you, and columbines: there's rue for you: there's a daisy: — I would give you some violets, but they withered all when my father died."

The minute knowledge that Shakespeare had of plants and flowers, and the loving appreciation

with which he describes pastoral scenery, are
explained to the rambler in Stratford, by all that
he sees and hears. There is a walk across the
fields to Shottery — which the poet must often
have taken, in the days of his courtship of Anne
Hathaway — whereon the feet of the traveller are
buried in wild flowers and furrow weeds. The
high road to the hamlet, also, passes through
rich meadows, and lands teeming with grain,
flecked everywhere with those brilliant scarlet
poppies which are so radiant and so bewitching in
the English landscape. To have grown up amidst
such surroundings, and, above all, to have experi-
enced amidst them the passion of love, must have
been, with Shakespeare, the intuitive acquire-
ment of most ample and most specific knowledge
of their manifold beauties. It would be hard to
find a sweeter rustic retreat than Anne Hathaway's
cottage is, even now. The tall trees embower it;
and over its porches, and all along its picturesque,
irregular front, and on its thatch-roof, the woodbine and the ivy climb, and there are wild roses
and the maiden's blush. For the young poet's
wooing no place could be fitter than this! He
would always remember it with tender joy. They
show you, in that cottage, an old settle, by the
fireside, whereon the lovers may have sat together;
and in the rude little chamber next the roof, an
antique, carved bedstead, which Anne Hathaway
once owned. This, it is thought, continued to be

Anne's home, for many years of her married life — her husband being absent in London, and sometimes coming down to visit her, at Shottery. "He was wont," says Aubrey, "to go to his native country once a year." The last surviving descendant of the Hathaway family — Mrs. Taylor — lives in the house now, and welcomes with homely hospitality the wanderers, from all lands, who seek — in a sympathy and reverence most honourable to human nature! — the shrine of Shakespeare's love. There is one such wanderer who will never forget the parting pressure of this good woman's hand, and who has never parted with her farewell gift of woodbine and roses from the porch of Anne Hathaway's cottage.

In England it is living, more than writing about it, that is esteemed by the best persons. They prize good writing, of course; but they prize noble living far more. This is an ingrained principle and not an artificial habit, and this principle, doubtless, was as potent in Shakespeare's age as it is to-day. Nothing could be more natural than that this great writer should think less of his works than of the establishment of his home. He would desire, having won his fortune, to dwell in his native place, to enjoy the companionship and esteem of his neighbours, to participate in their pleasures, to help them in their troubles, to aid in the improvement and embellishment of the town, to deepen his hold upon the affections of all around him, and to feel that, at last, honoured and lamented, his ashes would be laid in the village church where he had worshipped —

> "Among familiar names to rest,
> And in the places of his youth."

It was in 1597, about ten years after he went to London, that the poet began to buy property in Stratford, and it was about eight years after his first purchase that he finally settled there, at New Place. This mansion, as all readers know, was altered by Sir Hugh Clopton, who owned it about the middle of the eighteenth century, and was destroyed by the Rev. Mr. Gastrell, in 1757. There is a modern edifice on the estate now; but the grounds, which have been reclaimed, — chiefly through the zeal of Mr. Halliwell, — are laid out according to the model they are supposed to have presented when Shakespeare owned them. His lawn, his orchard, and his garden are indicated; and the grandson of his mulberry is growing on the very spot where that famous tree once flourished. You can see a part of the foundations of the old house. It seems to have had gables, and, no doubt, it was made of stone, and fashioned with the beautiful curves and broken lines of the Tudor architecture. They show, upon the lawn, a stone, of considerable size, which surmounted its door. The site — still the most commodious in Stratford — is on the corner of

High street and Chapel street; and on the opposite corner stands now, as it has stood for eight hundred years, the chapel of the Holy Cross, with square, dark tower, and fretted battlement, and arched casements, and Norman porch — one of the most romantic and picturesque churches in England. It was easy, when standing on that storied spot, to fancy Shakespeare, in the gloaming of a summer day, strolling on the lawn, beneath his elms, and listening to the soft and solemn music of the chapel organ; or to think of him as stepping forth from his study, in the late and lonesome hours of the night, and pausing to "count the clock," or note "the exhalations whizzing in the air."

The funeral train of Shakespeare, on that dark day when it moved from New Place to Stratford Church, had but a little way to go. The river, surely, must have seemed to hush its murmurs, the trees to droop their branches, the sunshine to grow dim — as that sad procession passed! His grave is under the grey pavement of the chancel, within the rail, and his wife and two daughters are buried beside him. The pilgrim who reads, upon the grave-stone itself, those rugged lines of grievous entreaty and awful imprecation which guard the poet's rest, feels no doubt that he is listening to his living voice — for he has now seen the enchanting beauty of the place, and he has now felt what passionate affection it can inspire.

Feeling and not manner would naturally have commanded that sudden agonized supplication and threat. Nor does such a pilgrim doubt, when gazing on the painted bust, above the grave, — made by Gerard Johnson, stone-cutter, — that he beholds the authentic face of Shakespeare. It is not the heavy face of the portraits that represent it. There is a rapt, transfigured quality in it, which these do not convey. It is thoughtful, austere, and yet benign. Shakespeare was a hazel-eyed man, with auburn hair, and the colours that he wore were scarlet and black. Being painted, and also being set up at a considerable height on the church wall, the bust does not disclose what is sufficiently perceptible in a cast from it — that it is, in fact, the copy of a mask from the dead face. One of the cheeks is a little swollen, and the tongue is very slightly protruded, and is caught between the lips. It need not be said that the old theory — that the poet was not a gentleman of great consideration in his own time and place — falls utterly and forever from the mind, when you stand at his grave. No man could have a more honourable or sacred spot of sepulture; and while it illustrates the profound esteem of the community in which he lived, it testifies to the high religious character by which that esteem was confirmed. "I commend my soul into the hands of God, my Creator, hoping, and assuredly believing, through the only merits of

Jesus Christ, my Saviour, to be made partaker of life everlasting." So said Shakespeare, in his last Will, bowing in humble reverence the mightiest mind — as vast and limitless in the power to comprehend as to express! — that ever wore the garments of mortality.

Once again there is a sound of organ music, very low and soft, in Stratford Church, and the dim light, broken by the richly stained windows, streams across the dusky chancel, filling the still air with opal haze, and flooding those grey gravestones with its mellow radiance. Not a word is spoken; but, at intervals, the rustle of the leaves is audible, in a sighing wind. What visions are these, that suddenly fill the region! What royal faces of monarchs, proud with power, or pallid with anguish! What sweet, imperial women, gleeful with happy youth and love, or wide-eyed and rigid in tearless woe! What warriors, with serpent diadems, defiant of death and hell! The mournful eyes of Hamlet; the wild countenance of Lear; Ariel with his harp, and Prospero with his wand! Here is no death! All these, and more, are immortal shapes; and he that made them so, though his mortal part be but a handful of dust in yonder crypt, is a glorious angel beyond the stars!

VIII.

A GLIMPSE OF FRANCE.

PARIS, August 1st, 1877. — It was a beautiful afternoon in July when first I saw the shores of France. The British Channel — a most distressful water when rough — had been in unusual pleasure, like King Duncan in the play, so that "observation with extended view," could look with interest, and without nausea, on the Norman coast, as it rose into sight across the surges. This coast seemed like the Palisade bank of the Hudson River, and prompted thoughts of home. It is high and precipitous, and on one of its windy hills a little chapel is perched, in picturesque loneliness, to the east of the stone harbour into which the arriving steamer glides. At Dieppe, as at most of the Channel ports, a long pier projects into the sea, and this was thronged with spectators, as our boat steamed up to her moorings. The ride from Dieppe to Paris is charming. The road passes through Rouen and up the Valley of the Seine. The sky that day was as blue and sunny as ever it is in brilliant America; the air was soft and cool; and the fields of Normandy were lovely with rich colour, and generous with abundance of golden crops. Now and then we passed little hamlets, made up of thatched cottages clustered around a tiny church, with its sad, quaint place of graves. Sheaves of wheat were stacked, in careless piles, in the meadows. Rows of the tall, lithe Lombardy poplar — so like the willowy girls of France — flashed by, and rows of the tremulous silver-leaved maple. Sometimes I saw rich bits of garden ground, gorgeous with geraniums and with many of the wild flowers (neglected, for the most part, in other countries), which the French know so well how to cultivate and train. In some fields the reapers were at work; in others women were guiding the plough; in others the sleek cattle and shaggy sheep were couched in repose, or busy with the herbage; and through this smiling land the Seine flowed peacefully down, shining like burnished silver. At Rouen I caught a glimpse of the round tower and two spires of the famous cathedral which is there — esteemed one of the best pieces of Gothic architecture in Europe; and I thought of Corneille, who was there born, and of Jean Darc, who was there burned. Just beyond Rouen, on the eastern bank of the Seine, the hills take, and for many miles preserve, the shape of natural fortifications. Zigzag pathways wind up the faces of these crags. A chapel crowns one of the loftiest summits. Cottages nestle in the vales below. A few gaunt wind-mills stretch forth their arms, upon the distant hills. Every rood of the land is cultivated; and here, as in England, the scarlet poppies brighten the green, while cosey hedge-rows make the landscape comfortable to the fancy, as well as pretty to the eye, with a sense of human companionship.

In the gloaming we glided into Paris, and before I had been there two hours I was driving in the Champs Elysées and thinking of the Arabian Nights. Nobody can know, without seeing them, how glorious and imperial the great features of Paris are. My first morning there was a Sunday, and it was made beautiful beyond expression by sunshine, the singing of birds, the strains of music from passing bands, and the many sights and sounds which in every direction bespoke the cheerfulness of the people. I went that day to a fête in the Bois de Vincennes, where from noon till midnight a great throng took its pleasure, in the most orderly, simple, and child-like manner, and where I saw a "picture in little" of the manners of the French. It was a peculiar pleasure, while in Paris, to rise at a very early hour and stroll through the markets of St. Honoré, in which flowers have at least an equal place with more substantial necessities of life, and where order and neatness are made perfect. It was impressive, also, to walk in the gardens of the Tuileries, in those lonely morning hours, and to muse and moralize over the downfall of the dynasty of Napoleon. These gardens, formerly the private grounds of the Emperor, are now opened to the public; and streams of labourers, clothed in their blue blouses, pour through them every day. They are rapidly rebuilding that part of the Tuileries which was destroyed by the Commune; and, in fact, though only six years have passed since [1871] the last revolution devastated this capital, but little trace remains of the ravages of that wild time. The Arc de Triomphe stands, in solemn majesty: the Column Vendôme towers toward the sky; the golden figure seems still in act to fly, upon the top of the Column of the Bastile. I saw, in the church of Notre Dame, the garments — stained with blood and riddled with bullets — that were worn by the Archbishop of Paris, when he was murdered by the friends of Liberty, Equality, and Fraternity; and I saw, with enthusiastic admiration, and not without a strong impulse to tears, the great Panorama of the Siege of Paris, by F. Phillipoteaux, which was exhibited in the region of the Champs Elysées, and which is a marvel of faithful detail, true colour, spirited composition, and the action and suffering of war. But these were all the tokens that I chanced to see of the recent evil days of France.

The more interesting sights of Paris are associated with its older history and with the taste and luxury of its present period. Every person who visits it repairs presently to Les Invalides, to see the tomb of Napoleon Buonaparte. This is a structure that would inspire awe, even if it were not associated with that glittering name and that terrible memory. The gloom of the crypt in which it is sunk; the sepulchral character of the mysterious, emblematic figures which surround it — "staring right on, with calm, eternal eyes;" the grandeur of the dome which rises above it; and its own vast size and deathly shape — all these characteristics unite to make it a most impressive object, apart from the thrilling fact that in this great, red-sandstone coffin rest, at last, after the stormiest of all human lives, the ashes of the most vital man of action who has lived in modern times. I was deeply impressed, too, by the sight of the tombs of Voltaire and Rousseau, in the vaults beneath the Pantheon. No device more apposite or more startling could have been adopted than that which assails you on the front of Rousseau's tomb.

The door stands ajar, and out of it issues an arm and hand, in marble, grasping a torch. It was almost as if the dead had spoken with a living voice, to see that fateful symbol of a power of thought and passion which never can die — while human hearts remain human. There is a fine statue of Voltaire in the vault that holds his tomb. These mausoleums are merely commemorative. The body of Voltaire, at any rate, was at once destroyed with quicklime, when laid in the grave, at the Abbey of Celleries, so that it might not be cast out of consecrated ground. Other tombs of departed greatness I found in Père la Chaise. Molière and La Fontaine rest side by side. Racine is a neighbour to them. Talma, Auber, Rossini, De Musset, Desclée, and many other illustrious names, may here be read, in the letters of death. I came upon Rachel's tomb, in the Hebrew quarter of the cemetery. It is a tall, narrow, stone structure, with a grated door, over which the name of Rachel — and nothing else — is graven, in black letters. Looking in through the grating I saw a shelf on which were vases and flowers, and beneath it were fourteen immortelle wreaths. A few cards, left by mourners of the dead, or by pilgrims to this solemn shrine of genius and illustrious renown, were upon the floor. I ventured to add my own, humbly and reverently, to the names which thus gave homage to the memory of a great actress, and I gathered

a few leaves from the shrubbery that grows in front of her grave. It is a pity that this famous cemetery should be, as it is, comparatively destitute of flowers and grass. It contains a few avenues of trees; but, for the most part, it is a mass of ponderous tombs, crowded close together upon a hot hill-side, traversed by little stony pathways sweltering in sun and dust. No sadder grave-yard was ever seen. All the acute anguish of remediless suffering, all the abject misery and arid desolation of hopeless grief, is symbolized in this melancholy place. Workmen were repairing the tomb of Héloïse and Abelard, and this, for a while, converted a bit of old romance to modern commonness. Still, I saw this tomb, and it was elevating to think that there may be

" . . . . which are things,
. . . . . which do not deceive."

The most gorgeous modern building in Paris is, undoubtedly, the Opera House. They are opening a street in front of this noble edifice, so as to place it at the end of yet another vista — as the usage is, in this magnificent city. There is no building in America that can vie with it in ornate splendour. We do but scant justice to the solid qualities in the French character. Grant that the character is mercurial; yet it contains elements of stupendous intensity and power; and this you feel, as perhaps you may never have felt it before.

when you look at such works as the Opera House, the Pantheon, the Madeleine, the Invalides, the Louvre, the Luxembourg, and the stone embankments which, for miles, hem in the Seine on both its sides. The grandest old building in Paris — also a living witness to French power and purpose — is the church of Notre Dame. It will not displace, in the affectionate reverence of Americans, the glory of Westminster Abbey; but it will fill an equal place in their memory. Its arches are not so grand; its associations are not so near and dear. But it is so exceedingly beautiful in forms and in simplicity that no one can help loving it; and by reason of certain windings, skilfully devised, in its avenues, it is invested with more of the alluring attribute of mystery. Some of its associations, also, are especially startling. You may there see the chapel in which Mary Stuart was married to her first husband, then Dauphin of France, and in which Henry the Sixth, of England, was crowned; and you may stand on the very spot on which Napoleon Buonaparte invested himself with the imperial diadem — which, with his own hands, he placed on his own head. I climbed the tower of this famous cathedral, and, at the loftiest attainable height, pictured in fancy the awful closing scene of "The Hunchback of Notre Dame." That romance seemed the truth then, and Claude Frollo, Esmeralda, and Quasimodo were as real as Richelieu. There is a vine growing near the

A Glimpse of France.

bell-tower, and some children were at play there, on the stone platform. I went into the bell and smote upon it with a wooden mallet, and heard with delight its rich, melodious, soulful music. The four hundred steps are well worn that lead to the tower of Notre Dame. There are few places on earth so fraught with memories; few that so well repay the homage of a pilgrim from a foreign land.

IX.

ENGLISH HOME SENTIMENT.

THE elements of discontent and disturbance which are visible in English society are found, upon close examination, to be merely superficial. Underneath them there abides a sturdy, unshakeable, inborn love of England. These croakings, grumblings, and bickerings do but denote the process by which the body politic frees itself from the headaches and fevers that embarrass the national health. The Englishman and his country are one; and when the Englishman complains against his country it is not because he believes that either there is or can be a better country elsewhere, but because his instinct of justice and order makes him crave perfection in his own. Institutions and principles are, with him, by nature, paramount to individuals; and individuals only possess importance — and that conditional on abiding rectitude — who are their representatives. Everything is done in England to promote the permanence and beauty of the home; and the permanence and beauty of the home, by a natural reaction, augment in the English people solidity of character and peace of life. They do not dwell in a perpetual fret and fume as to the acts, thoughts, and words of other races: for the English there is absolutely no public opinion outside of their own land; they do not live for the sake of working, but they work for the sake of living; and, as the necessary preparations for living have long since been completed, their country is at rest. This, it seemed to me, is the secret of England's first, and continuous, and last, and all-pervading charm and power for the stranger — the charm and power to soothe. As long as the world lasts England will be England still.

The efficacy of endeavouring to make a country a united, comfortable, and beautiful home for all its inhabitants, — binding every heart to the land by the same tie that binds every heart to the fireside, — is something well worthy to be considered, equally by the practical statesman and the contemplative observer. That way, assuredly, lies the welfare of the human race, and all the tranquillity that human nature — warped as it is by sin — will ever permit to this world. This endeavour has, through long ages, been steadily pursued in England, and one of its results — which is also one of its indications — is the vast accumulation of what may be called home treasures, in the city of London. The mere enumeration of them would fill large volumes. The description of them could not be completed in a life-time. It was this copiousness of historic wealth and poetic association, combined with the flavour of character and the sentiment of monastic repose, that bound Dr. Johnson to Fleet street, and made Charles Lamb such an inveterate lover of the town. Except it be to correct a possible insular narrowness, there can be no need that the Londoner should travel. Glorious sights, indeed, await him, if he journeys no further away than Paris ; but, aside from ostentation, luxury, gaiety, and excitement, Paris will give him nothing that he may not find at home. The great cathedral of Notre Dame will awe him; but not more than his own Westminster Abbey. The grandeur and beauty of La Madeleine will enchant him; but not more than the massive solemnity and stupendous magnificence of St. Paul's. The embankments of the Seine will satisfy his taste, with their symmetrical solidity; but he will not deem them superior, in any respect, to the embankments of the Thames. The Pantheon, the Hotel des

Invalides, the Luxembourg, the Louvre, the
Tribunal of Commerce, the Opera House,—all
these will dazzle and delight his eyes,
his remembrances of history, and firing
imagination of great events and persons; but
all these will fail to displace in his esteem the
grand Palace of Westminster, so stately in its
simplicity, so strong in its perfect grace! He
will ride through the exquisite Park of Monceau
— one of the loveliest spots in France — and so
onward to the Bois de Boulogne, with its sumptuous pomp of foliage, its romantic green vistas,
its multitudinous winding avenues, its hill-side
hermitage, its cascades, and its affluent lakes,
whereon the white swans beat the water with
their gladsome wings; but his soul will still turn,
with unshaken love and loyal preference, to the
sweetly sylvan solitudes of the Gardens of Kew.
He will marvel, in the museums of the Louvre,
the Luxembourg, and Cluny; and, doubtless, he
will freely concede that in paintings, whether
ancient or modern, the French display is larger
and finer than the English; but he will still
vaunt the British Museum as peerless throughout
the world, and he will still prize his National
Gallery, with its originals of Hogarth, Reynolds,
Gainsborough, and Turner, its spirited, tender,
and dreamy Murillos, and its matchless gems
of Rembrandt. He will admire, at the Théâtre
Français, the somewhat unimaginative and photo-

graphic perfection of French acting; but he will
be apt to reflect that English dramatic art, if
it often lacks finish, sometimes possesses nature;
and he will certainly perceive that the play-house
itself is not to be compared with either Her
Majesty's Theatre or Covent Garden. He will
luxuriate in the Champs Elysées, in the sú-
perb Boulevards, in the glittering pageant of precious jewels that blazes in the Rue de Paix and
the Palais Royal, and in that gorgeous panorama
of shop-windows for which the French capital is
unrivaled and famous; and he will not deny that,
as to brilliancy of aspect, Paris is prodigious and
unequaled — the most radiant of cities — the very
male sapphire in the crown of King Saul! But,
when all is seen, either that Louis the Fourteenth
created or Buonaparte pillaged, — when he has
taken his last walk in the gardens of the Tuileries,
and mused, at the foot of the statue of Cæsar, on
that Titanic strife of monarchy and democracy, of
which France seems destined to be the perpetual
theatre, — sated with the glitter of showy opulence, and tired with the whirl of frivolous life, he
will gladly and gratefully turn again to his
sombre, mysterious, thoughtful, restful old London; and, like the Syrian captain, though in the
better spirit of truth and right, declare that Abana
and Pharpar, rivers of Damascus, are better than
all the waters of Israel.

X.

LONDON NOOKS AND CORNERS.

THOSE persons upon whom the spirit of the past has power — and it has not power upon every mind! — are aware of the mysterious charm that invests certain familiar spots and objects, in all old cities. London, to observers of this class, is a never-ending delight. Modern cities, for the most part, reveal a definite and rather a common-place design. Their main avenues are parallel. Their shorter streets bisect their main avenues. They are diversified with rectangular squares. Their configuration, in brief, suggests the sapient, utilitarian forethought of the land-surveyor and civil engineer. The ancient British Capital, on the contrary, is the expression

— slowly and often narrowly made — of many thousands of characters. It is a city that has happened — and the stroller through the old part of it comes continually upon the queerest imaginable alleys, courts, and nooks. Not far from Drury Lane Theatre, for instance, hidden away in a clump of dingy houses, is a dismal little grave-yard — the same that Dickens has chosen, in his novel of "Bleak House," as the sepulchre of little Jo's friend, the first love of the unfortunate Lady Dedlock. It is a doleful spot, draped in the robes of faded sorrow, and crowded into the twilight of obscurity by the thick-clustering habitations of men. The Cripplegate church, — St. Giles's — a less lugubrious spot, and somewhat less difficult of access, is, nevertheless, strangely sequestered, so that it also affects the observant eye as equally one of the surprises of London. I saw it, for the first time, on a grey, sad Sunday, a little before twilight, and when the service was going on within its venerable, historic walls. The footsteps of John Milton were often on the threshold of the Cripplegate, and his grave is in the nave of that ancient church. A simple flat stone marks that sacred spot, and many a heedless foot tramples over that hallowed dust. From Golden Lane, which is close by, you can see the octagon tower of this church; and, as you walk from the place where Milton lived to the place where his ashes repose, you seem, with a solemn, awe-stricken emotion, to be actually following in his funeral train. The grave of Daniel De Foe, forever memorable as the author of the great and wonderful romance of "Robinson Crusoe," is also in the Cripplegate; and at its altar occurred the marriage of Oliver Cromwell. I remembered — as I stood there and conjured up that scene of golden joy and hope — the place of the Lord Protector's coronation in Westminster Hall; the place, still marked, in Westminster Abbey, where his body was buried; and old Temple Bar, on which [if not on Westminster Hall itself] his mutilated corse was finally exposed to the blind rage of the fickle populace. A little time — a very little time — serves to gather up equally the happiness and the anguish, the conquest and the defeat, the greatness and the littleness of human life, and to cover them all with silence.

But not always with oblivion. These quaint churches, and many other mouldering relics of the past, in London, are haunted with associations that never can perish out of remembrance. In fact, the whole of the old city impresses you as densely invested with an atmosphere of human experience, dark, sad, and lamentable. Walking, alone, in ancient quarters of it, after midnight — as I often did — I was aware of the oppressive sense of tragedies that have been acted, and misery that has been endured, in its dusky streets and melancholy houses. They do not err who say that the

spiritual life of man leaves its influence in the
physical objects by which he is surrounded.
Night-walks in London will teach you that, if they
teach you nothing else. I went more than once
into Brook street, Holborn, and traced the desolate
footsteps of poor Thomas Chatterton to the scene
of his self-murder and agonized, pathetic, deplor-
able death. It is more than a century [1770], since
that "marvellous boy" was driven to suicide by
neglect, hunger, and despair. They are tearing
down the houses on one side of Brook street now,
[1877]: it is doubtful which house was No. 39, in
the attic of which Chatterton died, and doubtful
whether it remains : his grave — a pauper's grave,
which was made in a work-house burial-ground, in
Shoe Lane, long since obliterated — is unknown :
but his presence hovers about that region ; his
strange and touching story tinges its squalour and
its commonness with the mystical moonlight of
romance ; and his name is blended with it forever.
On another night I walked from St. James's
Palace to Whitehall (the York Place of Cardinal
Wolsey), over the ground that Charles the First
must have traversed, on his way to the scaffold.
The story of the murder of that king, always sorrow-
ful to remember, is very grievous to consider, when
you realize, upon the actual scene of his ordeal and
death, his exalted fortitude and his bitter agony.
It seemed as if I could almost hear his voice, as it
sounded on that fateful morning, asking that his

body might be more thickly clad, lest, in the cold,
January air, he should shiver, and so, before the
eyes of his enemies, should seem to be trembling
with fear. The Puritans, having brought this
poor man to the place of execution, kept him in
suspense from early morning till after two o'clock
in the day, while they debated over a proposition
to spare his life — upon any condition they might
choose to make — which had been sent to them by
his son, Prince Charles. Old persons were alive
in London, not very long ago, who remembered
having seen, in their childhood, the window, in
the end of Whitehall, through which the doomed
monarch walked forth to the block. It was long
ago walled up, and the palace has undergone
much alteration since the days of the Stuarts; but
the spot, in the rear of Whitehall, where the king
was butchered, is marked to this day, in a manner
most tenderly significant. A bronze statue of
his son, James the Second, stands in this place.
It is by Roubiliac (whose marbles are numerous, in
the Abbey and elsewhere in London, and whose
grave is in St. Martin's Church), and it is one of
the most graceful works of that spirited sculptor.
The figure is slender, elegant, and beautifully
modelled. The face is downcast and full of grief
and reproach. The right hand points, with a
truncheon, toward the earth. It is impossible to
mistake the ruminant, melancholy meaning of this
memorial; and, equally, it is impossible to walk,

without both thought that instructs and emotion that elevates, through a city which thus abounds with traces of momentous incident and representative experience.

The literary pilgrim in London has this double advantage — that, while he communes with the past, he may enjoy in the present. Yesterday and to-day are commingled here, in a way that is almost ludicrous. When you turn from Roubiliac's statue of James, your eyes rest upon the retired house of Disraeli. If you walk past Whitehall, toward the Palace of Westminster, some friend may chance to tell you how the great Duke of Wellington walked there, in the feebleness of his age, from the Horse Guards to the House of Lords; and with what pleased complacency the old warrior used to boast of his skill in threading a crowded thoroughfare, — unaware that the police, acting by particular orders, were wont to protect his reverend person from errant cabs and pushing pedestrians. As I strolled, one day, past Lambeth Palace, on the road to Dulwich, it happened that the palace gates were suddenly unclosed, and that His Grace the Archbishop of Canterbury — a little, fat, sleek prelate, in black garments — came riding forth, on horseback, from this Episcopal residence, and pranced away toward the House of Lords. It is the same arched gateway through which, in other days, passed out the stately train of Wolsey. It is the same towered palace that Queen Elizabeth must have looked upon (and that was the last civic habitation she could have seen, upon the Surrey side of the Thames), as her barge swept past, on its watery track to Richmond. It is forever associated with the memory of the great Thomas Cromwell. In the church, hard by, rest the ashes of men distinguished in the most diverse directions — Ducrow, the equestrian actor; Jackson, the clown; and Tennison, the archbishop, the "honest, prudent, labourious, and benevolent" primate of William the Third, who was thought worthy to succeed in office the illustrious Tillotson. The cure of souls is sought here with just as vigourous energy as when Tillotson wooed by his goodness and charmed by his matchless eloquence. Not a great distance from this spot you come upon the college at Dulwich, that Edward Alleyn founded, in the time of Shakespeare, and that still subsists, upon the old actor's endowment. It is said that Alleyn — who was a man of fortune, and whom a contemporary epigram styles the best actor of his day — gained the most of his money by the exhibition of bears. But, howsoever gained, he made a good use of it. His tomb is in the centre of the college. Here may be seen one of the rarest picture-galleries in England. One of the cherished paintings in this collection is the famous portrait, by Sir Joshua Reynolds, of Mrs. Siddons as the Tragic Muse — remarkable for its colour, and splendidly expositive of the boldness of feature, brilliancy of countenance, and stately grace of posture for which its original was distinguished. Another represents two renowned beauties of their day—the Linley sisters—who became Mrs. Sheridan and Mrs. Tickel. You do not wonder, as you look upon these fair faces, sparkling with health, arch with merriment, lambent with sensibility, and soft with goodness and feeling, that Sheridan should have fought duels, for such a prize as the lady of his love; or that these fascinating creatures, favoured alike by the Graces and the Muse, should, in their gentle lives, have been, "like Juno's swans, coupled and inseparable." Mary, Mrs. Tickel, died first; and Moore, in his "Life of Sheridan," has preserved a lament for her, written by Eliza, Mrs. Sheridan, which — for deep, true sorrow, and melodious eloquence — is almost worthy to be named with Thomas Tickel's monody on Addison, or Cowper's memorial lines on his mother's picture: —

> "Shall all the wisdom of the world combined
> Erase thy image, Mary, from my mind,
> Or bid me hope from others to receive
> The fond affection thou alone could'st give?
> Ah no, my best beloved, thou still shalt be
> My friend, my sister, all the world to me!"

Precious also among the gems of the Dulwich gallery are certain excellent specimens of the gentle, dreamy style of Murillo. The pilgrim passes on, by a short drive, to Sydenham, and dines at the

Crystal Palace — and still he finds the faces of the past and the present confronted, in a manner that is almost comic. Nothing could be more aptly representative of the practical, showy phase of the spirit of to-day than is this enormous, opulent, and glittering "palace made of windows." Yet, I saw here the carriage in which Napoleon Buonaparte used to drive, at St. Helena — a vehicle as sombre and ghastly as were the broken fortunes of its death-stricken master; and, sitting at the next table to my own, I saw the son of Buonaparte's great defender, William Hazlitt.

It was a grey and misty evening. The plains below the palace terraces were veiled in shadow, through which, here and there, twinkled the lights of some peaceful villa. Far away the spires and domes of London, dimly seen, pierced the city's nightly pall of smoke. It was a dream too sweet to last. It ended when all the illuminations were burnt out; when the myriads of red and green and yellow stars had fallen; and all the silver fountains had ceased to play.

XI.

THE TOWER AND THE BYRON MEMORIAL.

LONDON, July 15th, 1877.—The Tower of London is degraded by being put to commonplace uses, and by being exhibited in a commonplace manner. They use the famous White Tower, now, as a store-house for arms, and it contains at this minute 102,000 guns, in perfect order, besides a vast collection of old armour and weapons. The arrangement of the latter was made by J. R. Planché, the dramatic author,—famous as an antiquarian and a herald. [This learned, able, brilliant, and honoured gentleman died, May 29th, 1880, aged 84 years.] Under his tasteful direction the effigies and gear of chivalry are displayed in such a way that the observer may trace the changes which war fashions have undergone, through the reigns of successive sovereigns of England, from the earliest period until now. A suit of armour worn by Henry the Eighth is shown, and also a suit worn by Charles the First. The suggestiveness of both figures is remarkable. In a room on the second floor of the White Tower they keep many gorgeous oriental weapons, and they show the cloak in which General Wolfe died, on the Plains of Abraham. It is a grey garment, to which the active moth has given a share of his personal attention. The most impressive objects to be seen here, however, are the block and axe that were used in beheading the traitor lords, Kilmarnock Lovat, and Balmerino, after the defeat of the Pretender, in 1745. The block is of ash, and there are big and cruel dents upon it, which show that it was made for use rather than ornament. It is harmless enough now, and this writer was allowed to place his head upon it, in the manner prescribed for the victims of decapitation. The door of Raleigh's bedroom is opposite to these baleful relics, and it is said that his "History of the World" was written in the room in which these implements are now such conspicuous objects of gloom. The whole place is gloomy and cheerless beyond expression, and great must have been the fortitude of the man who bore, in this grim solitude, a captivity of thirteen years — not failing to turn it to the best account, by producing a book so excellent for quaintness, philosophy, and eloquence. A ridiculous "beef-eater," arrayed in a dark tunic and trousers trimmed with red, and a black velvet hat trimmed with bows of blue and red ribbon, precedes each group of visitors, and drops information and h's, from point to point. "The 'ard fate of the Hurl of Hessex" was found to be a particularly fascinating topic with one of these functionaries; and very hard it was — for the listener as well as the language — when standing on the spot where that poor gentleman lost his life, by the mad spite of Queen Elizabeth and the treacherous enmity of Raleigh and Cecil, to hear his name so persecuted. This spot is in the centre of what was once the Tower Green, and it is marked with a brass plate, naming Anne Boleyn, and giving the date when she was there beheaded. They found her body in an elm-wood box, made to hold arrows, and it now rests, with the ashes of other noble sufferers, under the stones of the chapel of St. Peter, about fifty feet from the place of execution. The ghost of Anne Boleyn is said to haunt that part of the Tower where she lived, and it is likewise said that the spectre of Lady Jane Grey was seen, not long ago, on the anniversary of the day of her execution [Obt. 1554], to glide out upon a balcony adjacent to the room she is believed to have occupied, at the last of her wasted, unfortunate life. It could serve no good purpose to relate the particulars of these visitations; but nobody doubts them

—while he is in the Tower. It is a place of mystery and horror, notwithstanding all that the practical spirit of to-day can do, an I has done, to make it common and to cheapen its grim glories.

The Byron Memorial Loan Collection, which was displayed at the Albert Memorial Hall, did not attract what, in America, would be considered much attention. Yet it was a vastly impressive show of relics. The catalogue names seventy-four objects, and thirty-nine designs for a monument to Byron. The design which has been chosen presents a seated figure, of the young sailor-boy type. The right hand supports the chin; the left, resting on the left knee, holds an open book and a pencil. The dress consists of a loose shirt, open at the collar and down the bosom, a flowing neck-cloth, and wide, sailor-like trousers. Byron's dog, Boatswain—commemorated in the well-known epitaph,

"To mark a friend's remains these stones arise,
I never knew but one, and here he lies"—

is shown, in effigy, at the poet's feet. The treatment of the subject, in this model, certainly deserves to be called free, but the general effect of the work is finical. The statue will, probably, be popular; but it will give no adequate idea of the man. Byron was both massive and intense; and this image is no more than the usual hero of nautical romance. [It was dedicated, in London, in May, 1880].

It was the relic department, however, and not the statuary, that more attracted notice. The relics were exhibited in three glass cases, exclusive of large portraits. It is impossible, by written words, to make the reader — supposing him to revere this great poet's genius, and to care for his memory — feel the thrill of emotion that was aroused, by actual sight, and almost actual touch, of objects so intimately associated with the living Byron. Five pieces of his hair were shown, one of which was cut off, after his death, by Captain Trelawny — the remarkable gentleman who says that he uncovered the legs of the corse, in order to ascertain the nature and extent of their deformity. All these locks of hair are faded, and all present a mixture of grey and brown. Byron's hair was not, seemingly, of a fine texture, and it appears to have turned grey early in life. These tresses were lent to the exhibition, by Lady Dorchester, Mr. John Murray, the Rev. H. M. Robinson, D. D., and E. J. Trelawny. A strangely interesting memorial was a little locket of plain gold, shaped like a heart, which Byron habitually wore. Near to this was the crucifix found in his room at Missolonghi, after his death. It is about ten inches long, and is made of ebony. A small bronze figure of Christ is displayed upon it, and at the feet of this figure are cross-bones and a skull, of the same metal. A glass beaker, which Byron gave to his butler, in 1815, attracted attention by its portly size, and, to the profane fancy, hinted that his lordship had formed a liberal estimate of the butler's powers of suction. Four articles of head-gear a prominent place in one of the cabinets. are helmets that Byron wore when he was in Greece, in 1824 — and very queer must have been his ... when he wore them. One is light blue, the other dark green; both are faded; both ... fierce with brass ornaments, and barbaric ... brass scales like those of a snake. A come-... object is the poet's "boarding-cap."— a leathern ... turned up with green velvet and studded ... h brass nails. Many small articles of Byron's property were scattered through the cases. A corpulent little silver watch, with Arabic numerals upon its face, and a meerschaum pipe, not much coloured, were among them. The cap that he sometimes wore, during the last years of his life, and that is depicted in the well-known sketch of him by Count D'Orsay, was exhibited, and so was D'Orsay's portrait. The cap is of green velvet, not much tarnished, and is surrounded by a gold band and faced by an ugly vizor. The face, in the sketch, is supercilious and cruel. A better and obviously truer sketch is that made by Cattermole, which also was in this exhibition. Strength in despair and a dauntless spirit that shines through the ravages of irremediable suffering are the qualities of this portrait; and they make it marvellously effective. Thorwaldsen's fine bust of Byron, made for Hobhouse, and also the celebrated Phillips portrait — which

Scott said was the best likeness of Byron ever painted — occupied places in this group. The copy of the New Testament which Lady Byron gave to her husband, and which he, in turn, presented to Lady Caroline Lamb, was there, and is a pocket volume, bound in black leather, with the inscription, "From a sincere and anxious friend," written, in a stiff, formal hand, across the fly-leaf. A gold ring that the poet constantly wore, and the collar of his dog Boatswain — a discoloured band of brass, with sharply jagged edges — should also be named, as among the most interesting of the relics.

But the most remarkable objects of all were the manuscripts. These comprise the original draft of the third canto of "Childe Harold," written on odd bits of paper, during Byron's journey from London to Venice, in 1816; the first draft of the fourth canto, together with a clean copy of it; the notes to "Marino Faliero;" the concluding stage directions — much scrawled and blotted — in "Heaven and Earth;" a document concerning the poet's matrimonial trouble; and about fifteen of his letters. The passages seen are those beginning "Since my young days of passion, joy, or pain;" "To bear unhurt what time cannot abate:" and, in canto fourth, the stanzas from 118 to 129 inclusive. The writing is free and strong, and it still remains entirely legible, although the paper is yellow with age. Altogether, these relics were touchingly significant of the strange, dark, sad career of a wonderful man. Yet, as already said, they attracted but little notice. The memory of Byron seems darkened, as with the taint of lunacy. "He did strange things," one Englishman said to me; "and there was something queer about him." The London house, in which he was born, in Holles street, Cavendish square, is marked with a tablet — according to a custom instituted by a society of arts — and that is about all the visible memorial to him in London. The houses in which he lived, No. 8 St. James street, near the old Palace, and No. 13 Piccadilly terrace, are not marked. The latter is now a chemist's shop, while the house of his birth is occupied by a descendant of Elizabeth Fry, the "philanthropist."

The custom of marking the houses associated with great names is, obviously, a good one, and it ought to be adopted in our country. Two buildings here, one in Westminster and one in the grounds of the South Kensington Museum, bear the name of Franklin; and I also saw memorial tablets to Dryden and Burke, in Gerrard street, to Mrs. Siddons, in Baker street, to Sir Joshua Reynolds, in Leicester square, opposite to the Alhambra, to Garrick, in the Adelphi terrace, to Louis Napoleon, and to many other renowned individuals. The room that Sir Joshua occupied as a studio is now an auction mart. The stone stairs leading up to it are much worn, but remain as they were when, it may be imagined, Burke, Johnson, Goldsmith, Langton, Beauclerk, and Boswell walked there, on many a festive night in the old times.

It is a breezy, slate-coloured evening in July. I look from the window of a London house which fronts a spacious park. Those great elms, which Birket Foster draws so well, and which, in their wealth of foliage and irregular and pompous expanse of limb, are finer than all other trees of their class, fill the prospect, and nod and murmur in the wind. Through a rift in their heavy-laden boughs is visible a long vista of green field, in which some children are at play. Their laughter, and the rustle of leaves, with now and then the click of a horse's hoofs upon the road near by, make up the music of this summer eve. The sky is a little overcast, but not gloomy. As I muse upon this delicious scene, the darkness slowly gathers, the stars come out, and presently the moon rises, and blanches the meadow with silver light. This has been the English summer, with scarce a touch of either heat or storm.

XII.

WESTMINSTER ABBEY.

IT is strange that the life of the past, in its unfamiliar remains and fading traces, should so far surpass the life of the present, in impressive force and influence. Human characteristics, although manifested under widely different conditions, were the same in old times that they are now. It is not in them, surely, that we are to seek for the mysterious charm which hallows ancient objects and the historical antiquities of the world. There is many a venerable, weather-stained church in London, at sight of which your steps falter and your thoughts take a wistful, melancholy turn — though then you may not know either who built it, or who has worshipped in it, or what dust of the dead is mouldering in its vaults. The spirit which thus instantly possesses and controls you is not one of association, but is inherent in the place. Time's shadow on the works of man, like moonlight on a landscape, gives only graces to the view — tingeing them, the while, with sombre sheen — and leaves all blemishes in darkness. This may suggest the reason that relics of by-gone years so sadly please and strangely awe us, in the passing moment; or, it may be that we involuntarily contrast their apparent permanence with our own evanescent mortality, and so are dejected with a sentiment of dazed helplessness and solemn grief. This sentiment it is — allied to bereaved love and a natural wish for remembrance after death — that has filled Westminster Abbey, and many another holy mausoleum, with sculptured memorials of the departed; and this, perhaps, is the subtile power that makes us linger beside them, " with thoughts beyond the reaches of our souls."

When the gentle old angler Izaak Walton went into Westminster Abbey to visit the grave of Casaubon, he scratched his initials on his friend's monument — where the record, "I. W., 1658," may still be read, by the stroller in Poets' Corner. One might well wish to follow that example, and even thus to associate his name with the great cathedral. And not in pride, but in humble reverence! Here, if anywhere on earth, self-assertion is rebuked and human eminence set at naught. Among all the impressions that crowd upon the mind, in this wonderful place, that which oftenest recurs and

longest remains, is the impression of man's
insignificance. This is salutary, but it is
dark. There can be no enjoyment of the Abbey
till, after much communion with the spirit of the
place, your soul is soothed by its beauty rather than
overwhelmed by its majesty, and your mind ceases
from the vain effort to grasp and interpret its tremendous
meaning. You cannot long endure, and
you never can express, the sense of grandeur that
is inspired by Westminster Abbey; but, when at
length its shrines and tombs and statues become
familiar, when its chapels, aisles, arches, and cloisters
are grown companionable, and you can stroll
and dream undismayed " through rows of warriors
and through walks of kings," there is no limit to
the pensive memories they awaken and the poetic
fancies they prompt. In this church are buried,
amidst generations of their nobles and courtiers,
fourteen monarchs of England — beginning with
the Saxon Sebert and ending with George the Second.
Fourteen queens rest here, and many children
of the royal blood who never came to the
throne. Here, confronted in a haughty rivalry of
solemn pomp, rise the equal tombs of Elizabeth
Tudor and Mary Stuart. Queen Eleanor's dust is
here (who still slays Fair Rosamond in the ancient
ballad), and here, too, is the dust of the grim
Queen Mary. In one little nook you may pace,
with but half a dozen steps, across the graves of
Charles the Second, William and Mary, and Queen

Anne and her consort Prince George. At the tomb of Henry the Fifth you may see the helmet, shield, and saddle which were worn by that valiant young king, at Agincourt; and close by — on the tomb of Margaret Woodeville, daughter of Edward the Fourth — the sword and shield that were borne, in royal state, before the great Edward the Third, 500 years ago. The princes whom Richard murdered in the Tower are commemorated here, by an altar, set up by Charles the Second, whereon the inscription — blandly and almost humourously oblivious of the incident of Cromwell — states that it was erected in the thirtieth year of Charles's reign. Richard the Second, deposed and assassinated, is here entombed; and within a few feet of him are the relics of his uncle, the able and powerful Duke of Gloucester, whom so treacherously he ensnared, and betrayed to death. Here also, huge, rough, and grey, is the marble sarcophagus of Edward the First, which, when opened, more than a hundred years ago, disclosed the skeleton of departed majesty, still perfect, wearing robes of gold tissue and crimson velvet, and having a crown on the head and a sceptre in the hand. So sleep, in jeweled darkness and gaudy decay, what once were monarchs! And all around are great lords, sainted prelates, famous statesmen, renowned soldiers, and illustrious poets. Burleigh, Pitt, Fox, Burke, Canning, Newton, Barrow, Wilberforce — names forever glorious! — are here enshrined in the grandest sepulchre on earth.

The interments that have been effected in and around the Abbey, since the remote age of Edward the Confessor, must number thousands; but only about 600 are named in the guide-books. In the south transept, which is Poets' Corner, rest Chaucer, Spenser, Drayton, Cowley, Dryden, Beaumont, Davenant, Prior, Gay, Congreve, Rowe, Dr. Johnson, Campbell, Macaulay, and Dickens. Memorials to many other poets and writers have been ranged on the adjacent walls and pillars; but these are among the authors that were actually buried in this place. Ben Jonson is not here, but — in an upright posture, it is said — under the north aisle of the Abbey; Addison is in the chapel of Henry the Seventh, at the foot of the monument of Charles Montague, the great Earl of Halifax; and Bulwer is in the chapel of Saint Edmund. Garrick, Sheridan, Henderson, Cumberland, Handel, Parr, Sir Archibald Campbell, and the once so mighty Duke of Argyle are almost side by side; while, at a little distance, sleep Anne of Cleves, the divorced wife of Henry the Eighth, and Anne Neville, the murdered Queen of Richard the Third. Betterton and Spranger Barry are in the cloisters — where may be read, in four little words, the most touching of all the epitaphs in the Abbey: "Jane Lister — dear child." There are no monuments to either Byron, Shelley, Swift, Pope, Bolingbroke, Keats, Cowper, Moore, Young, or Coleridge: but Mason and Shadwell are commemorated; and Barton Booth is splendidly inurned; while hard by, in the cloisters, a place was found for Mrs. Cibber, Tom Brown, Anne Bracegirdle, and Aphra Behn. The destinies have not always been stringently fastidious as to the admission of lodgers to this sacred ground. The pilgrim is startled by some of the names that he finds in Westminster Abbey, and pained by reflection on the absence of some that he will seek in vain. Yet he will not fail to moralize, as he strolls in Poets' Corner, upon the inexorable justice with which time repudiates fictitious reputations, and twines the laurel on only the worthiest brows. In well-nigh five hundred years of English literature there have lived only about a hundred and ten poets whose names survive in any needed chronicle; and not all of these possess life, outside of the library. To muse over the literary memorials in the Abbey is also to think upon the seeming caprice of chance with which the graves of the British poets have been scattered far and wide throughout the land. Gower, Fletcher, and Massinger (to name but a few of them) rest in Southwark; Sydney, Donne, and Butler, in St. Paul's; More (his head, that is, while his body moulders in the Tower Chapel), at Canterbury; Drummond in Lasswade church; Dorset at Withiam, in Sussex; Waller at Beaconsfield; Wither in the church of the Savoy; Milton in the church of the Cripplegate; Swift at Dublin, in St. Patrick's Cathedral; Young at Welwyn; Pope at Twicken-

ham; Thomson at Rich[...]; [...] at Stoke-Pogis; Watts in Bunhill[...]; [...]s at Chichester; Cowper in Dereham church; Goldsmith in the garden of the Temple; Savage at Bristol; Burns at Dumfries; Rogers at Hornsey; Crabbe at Trowbridge; Scott in Dryburgh Abbey; Coleridge at Highgate; Byron in Hucknall church, near Nottingham; Moore at Bromham; Montgomery at Sheffield; Heber at Calcutta; Southey in Crossthwaite church-yard, near Keswick; Wordsworth and Hartley Coleridge side by side in the church-yard of Grasmere; and Clough at Florence — whose lovely words may here speak for all of them:

> "One port, methought,
>   Alike they sought,
> One purpose held, where'er they fare:
>   O bounding breeze,
>   O rushing seas.
> At last, at last, unite them there!"

But it is not alone in the great Abbey that the rambler in London is impressed by poetic antiquity and touching historic association — always presuming that he has been a reader of English literature, and that his reading has sunk into his mind. Little things, equally with great ones, commingled in a medley, luxuriant and delicious, so people the memory of such a pilgrim that all his walks will be haunted. The London of to-day, to be sure (as may be seen in Macaulay's famous Third Chapter, and in Scott's "Fortunes of Nigel"), is very little like even the London of Charles the Second, when the great fire had destroyed eighty-nine churches and 13,000 houses, and when what is now Regent street was a rural solitude, in which sportsmen sometimes shot the woodcock. Yet, though much of the old capital has vanished, and more of it has been changed, many remnants of its historic past exist, and many of its streets and houses are fraught with a delightful, romantic interest. It is not forgotten that sometimes the charm resides in the eyes that see, quite as much as in the object that is seen. The storied spots of London may not be appreciable by all who look upon them every day. The cab-drivers in Kensington may neither regard, nor even notice, the house in which Thackeray lived and died. The shop-keepers of old Bond street may, perhaps, neither care nor know that in this famous avenue was enacted the woful death-scene of Laurence Sterne. The Bow-street runners are quite unlikely to think of Will's Coffee House, and Dryden, or Button's, and Addison, as they pass the sites of those vanished haunts of wit and revelry in the days of Queen Anne. The fashionable lounger through Berkeley square, when perchance he pauses at the corner of Bruton street, will not discern Colley Cibber, in wig and ruffles, standing at the parlour window and drumming with his hands on the frame. The casual passenger, halting at the Tavistock, will not remember that this was once Macklin's Ordinary, and so conjure up the iron visage and ferocious aspect of the first great Shylock of the British stage, formally obsequious to his guests, or striving to edify them, despite the banter of the volatile Foote, with discourse upon "the Causes of Duelling in Ireland." The Barbican does not to every one summon the austere memory of Milton; nor Holborn raise the melancholy shade of Chatterton; nor Tower Hill arouse the gloomy ghost of Otway; nor Hampstead lure forth the sunny figure of Steele and the passionate face of Keats; nor old Northampton Street suggest the burly presence of "rare Ben Jonson;" nor opulent Kensington revive the stately head of Addison; nor a certain window in Wellington Street, reveal, in fancy's picture, the rugged lineaments and splendid eyes of Dickens. Yet London never disappoints; and, for him who knows and feels its history, these associations, and hundreds like to these, make it populous with noble or strange or pathetic figures, and diversify the aspect of its vital present with pictures of an equally vital past. Such a wanderer discovers that, in this vast capital, there is literally no end to the themes that are to stir his imagination, touch his heart, and broaden his mind. Soothed already by the equable English climate and the lovely English scenery, he is aware now of an influence in the solid English city that turns his intellectual life to perfect tranquillity. He stands amidst achievements that are finished, careers that are consummated, great deeds that are done, great memories that are immortal; he views and comprehends the sum of all that is possible to human thought, passion, and labour; and then, — high over mighty London, above the dome of St. Paul's Cathedral, piercing the clouds, greeting the sun, drawing into itself all the tremendous life of the great city and all the meaning of its past and present, — the golden cross of Christ!

THE HOME OF SHAKESPEARE.

[Reprinted from Harper's Magazine, for May, 1870.]

Others abide our question. Thou art free.
We ask and ask: thou smilest and art still,
Out-topping knowledge. For the loftiest hill
That to the stars uncrowns his majesty,
Planting his steadfast footsteps in the sea,
Making the heaven of heavens his dwelling-place,
Spares but the cloudy border of his base
To the foiled searching of mortality.
And thou, who didst the stars and sunbeams know,
Self-schooled, self-scanned, self-honoured, self-secure,
Didst walk on earth unguessed at. Better so!
All pains the immortal spirit must endure,
All weakness that impairs, all griefs that bow,
Find their sole voice in that victorious brow.
                              —MATTHEW ARNOLD.

XIII.

THE HOME OF SHAKESPEARE.

IT is the everlasting glory of Stratford-upon-Avon that it was the birth-place of Shakespeare. In itself, although a pretty and charming spot, it is not, among English towns, either pre-eminently beautiful or exceptionally impressive. Situated in the heart of Warwickshire, which has been called "the garden of England," it nestles cosily in an atmosphere of tranquil loveliness, and is surrounded, indeed, with everything that soft and gentle rural scenery can afford, to soothe the mind and to nurture contentment. It stands upon a level plain, almost in the centre of the island, through which, between the low green hills that roll away on either side, the Avon flows downward to ancient Gloucester and the Severn. The country in its neighbourhood is under perfect cultivation, and for many miles around presents the appearance of a superbly appointed park. Portions of the land are devoted to crops and pasture; other portions are thickly wooded with oak, elm, willow, and chestnut; the meadows are intersected by hedges of the fragrant hawthorn, and the whole region smiles with flowers. Old manor-houses, half hidden among the trees, and thatched cottages embowered with roses, are sprinkled through the surrounding landscape; and all the roads which converge upon this point — from Warwick, Banbury, Bidford, Alcester, Evesham, Worcester, and many other contiguous towns — wind, in sun and shadow, through a sod of green velvet, swept by the cool, sweet winds of the English summer. Such felicities of situation and such accessories of beauty, however, are not unusual in England; and Stratford, were it not hallowed by association, though it might always hold a place among the pleasant memories of the traveller, would not have become a shrine for the homage of the world. To Shakespeare it owes its renown; from Shakespeare it derives the bulk of its prosperity. To visit Stratford is to tread with affectionate veneration in the footsteps of the poet. To write about Stratford is to write about Shakespeare.

More than three hundred years have passed since the birth of that colossal genius, and many changes must have occurred in his native town, within that period. The Stratford of Shakespeare's time was built principally of timber — as, indeed, it is now —

and contained about fourteen hundred inhabitants. To-day its population numbers upward of ten thousand. New dwellings have arisen where once were fields of wheat, glorious with the shimmering lustre of the scarlet poppy. The older buildings, for the most part, have been demolished or altered. Manufactories, chiefly of beer and of Shakespearean relics, have been stimulated into prosperous activity. The Avon has been spanned by a new bridge, of iron. The village streets have been levelled, swept, rolled, and garnished till they look like a Flemish drawing of the Middle Ages. Even the Shakespeare cottage, the ancient Tudor house in High street, and the two old churches — authentic and splendid memorials of a distant and storied past — have been "restored." If the poet could walk again through his accustomed haunts, though he would see the same smiling country round about, and hear, as of old, the ripple of the Avon murmuring in its summer sleep, his eyes would rest on scarce a single object that once he knew. Yet, there are the paths that Shakespeare often trod; there stands the house in which he was born; there is the school in which he was taught; there is the cottage in which he wooed his sweetheart, and in which he dwelt with her as his wife; there are the ruins and relics of the mansion in which he died; and there is the church that keeps his dust, so consecrated by the reverence of mankind

"That kings for such a tomb would wish to die."

In shape the town of Stratford somewhat resembles a large cross, which is formed by High street, running nearly north and south, and Bridge street, running nearly east and west. From these, which are main avenues, radiate many and devious branches. A few of the streets are broad and straight, but many of them, particularly on the water side, are narrow and circuitous. High and Bridge streets intersect each other at the centre of the town, and here stands the market-house; an ancient building, with belfry-tower and illuminated clock, facing eastward toward the old stone bridge, with fourteen arches, — the bridge that Sir Hugh Clopton built across the Avon in the reign of Henry the Seventh. From that central point a few steps will bring the traveller to the birth-place of Shakespeare. It is a little, two-story cottage of timber and plaster, on the north side of Henley street, in the western part of the town. It must have been, in its pristine days, much finer than most of the dwellings in its neighbourhood. The one-story house, with attic windows, was the almost invariable fashion of building, in all English country towns, till the seventeenth century. This cottage, besides its two stories, had dormer-windows above its roof, a pent-house over its door, and altogether was built and appointed in a manner both luxurious and substantial. Its age is unknown; but the history of Stratford reaches back to a period three hundred years antecedent to William the Conqueror, and fancy, therefore, is allowed the amplest room to magnify its antiquity. It was bought, or at all events occupied, by Shakespeare's father in 1555, and in it he resided till his death, in 1601, when it descended by inheritance to the poet. Such is the substance of the somewhat confused documentary evidence and of the emphatic tradition which consecrate this cottage as the house in which Shakespeare was born. The point, as is well known, has never been absolutely settled. John Shakespeare, the father, in 1564, was the owner not only of the house in Henley street, but of another in Greenhill street, and of still another at Ingon, about a mile and a half from Stratford, on the road to Warwick. William Shakespeare might have been born at either of these dwellings, and it is not impossible that several generations of the poet's worshippers have been dilating with emotion in the wrong place. Tradition, however, has sanctified the Henley-street cottage; and this, accordingly, as Shakespeare's cradle, will doubtless be piously guarded to a late posterity.

It has already survived serious perils and vicissitudes. By Shakespeare's will it was bequeathed to his sister Joan — Mrs. William Hart — to be held by her, under the yearly rent of twelvepence, during her life, and at her death to revert to his daughter Susanna and her descendants. His sister Joan appears to have been living there at the time of his decease, in 1616. She is known to have been living there in 1639 — twenty-three years later — and doubtless she resided there till her death, in 1646. The estate then passed to Susanna — Mrs. John Hall — from whom in 1649 it descended to her grandchild, Lady Barnard, who left it to her kinsmen, Thomas and George Hart, grandsons of Joan. In this line of descent it continued — subject to many of those infringements which are incidental to poverty — till 1806, when William Shakespeare Hart, the seventh in collateral kinship from the poet, sold it to Thomas Court, from whose family it was at last purchased for the British nation. Meantime the property, which originally consisted of two tenements and a considerable tract of adjacent land, had, little by little, been curtailed of its fair proportions by the sale of its gardens and orchards. The two tenements — two in one, that is — had been subdivided. A part of the building became an inn — at first called "The Maidenhead," afterward "The Swan," and finally "The Swan and Maidenhead." Another part became a butcher's shop. The old dormer windows and the pent-house disappeared. A new brick casing was foisted upon the tavern end of the structure. In front of the butcher's shop appeared a sign announcing "William Shakespeare was born in this house. N. B. — A Horse and Taxed Cart to Let." Still later appeared another legend, vouching that "the immortal Shakespeare was born in this house." From 1793 till 1820 Thomas and Mary

Hornby, connections by marriage with the Harts, lived in the Shakespeare   w at length become the resort of litera   ms — . Hornby, who set up to be a   and wrote tragedy, comedy, and philosophy, took great delight in exhibiting its rooms to visitors. During the reign of this eccentric custodian the low ceilings and white-washed walls of its several chambers became covered with autographs, scrawled thereon by many enthusiasts, including some of the most famous persons in Europe. In 1820 Mary Hornby was requested to leave the premises. She did not wish to go. She could not endure the thought of a successor. "After me, the deluge." She was obliged to abdicate; but she conveyed away all the furniture and relics alleged to be connected with Shakespeare's family, and she hastily whitewashed the cottage walls. Only a small part of the wall of the upper room, the chamber in which "nature's darling" first saw the light, escaped this act of spiteful sacrilege. On the space behind its door may still be read many names, with dates affixed, ranging back from 1820 to 1792. Among them is that of Dora Jordan, the beautiful and fascinating actress, who wrote it there June 2, 1809. Much of Mary Hornby's whitewash, which chanced to be unsized, was afterward removed, so that her work of obliteration proved only in part successful. Other names have been added to this singular, chaotic scroll of worship. Byron, Scott, Thackeray, Kean, Tennyson, and Dickens are illustrious among the votaries here and thus recorded. The successors of Mary Hornby guarded their charge with pious care. The precious value of the old Shakespeare cottage grew more and more sensible to the English people. Washington Irving made his famous pilgrimage to Stratford, and recounted it in his beautiful "Sketch-Book." Yet it was not till Mr. Barnum, from the United States, arrived with a proposition to buy the Shakespeare house and convey it to America that the literary enthusiasm of Great Britain was made to take a practical shape; and this venerated and inestimable relic became, in 1847, a national possession. In 1856, John Shakespeare, of Worthington field, near Ashby-de-la-Zouch, gave £2,500 to preserve and restore it; and within the next two years, under the superintendence of Edward Gibbs, an architect of Stratford, it was isolated by the demolition of the cottages at its sides and in the rear, repaired wherever decay was visible, set in perfect order, and restored to its ancient self.

The builders of this house must have done their work thoroughly well, for, even after all these years of rough usage and of slow but incessant decline, the great timbers remain solid, the plastered walls are firm, the huge chimney-stack is as permanent as a rock, and the ancient flooring only betrays by the scooped-out aspect of its boards, and the high polish on the heads of the nails which fasten them down, that it belongs to a period of remote antiquity. The cottage stands close upon the margin of the street, according to ancient custom of building throughout Stratford; and, entering through a little porch, the pilgrim stands at once in that low-ceiled, flag-stoned room, with its wide fire-place, so familiar in prints of the chimney-corner of Shakespeare's youthful days. Within the fire-place, on either side, are seats fashioned in the brick-work; and here, as it is pleasant to imagine, the boy-poet often sat, on winter nights, gazing dreamily into the flames, and building castles in that fairy-land of fancy which was his celestial inheritance. Nothing else in this room detains attention, and you presently pass from it by a narrow, well-worn staircase to the chamber above, which is shown as the place of the poet's birth. An antiquated chair, of the sixteenth century, stands in the right-hand corner. At the left is a small fire-place, made in the rectangular form which is still usual. All around the walls are visible the great beams which are the frame-work of the building — beams of seasoned oak that will last forever. Opposite to the door of entrance is a three-fold casement (the original window) full of narrow panes of white glass scrawled all over with names that their worshipful owners have written with diamonds. The ceiling is so low that you can easily touch it with uplifted hand. A portion of it, about a yard square, is held in place by an intricate net-work of little laths. This room, and, indeed, the whole structure, is as polished and lustrous as any waxen, royal hall in the Louvre, and it impresses observation very much like old lace that has been treasured up in lavender or jasmine. These walls, which no one is now permitted to mar, were naturally the favourite scroll of the Shakespeare votaries of long ago. Every inch of the plaster bears marks of the pencil of reverence. Hundreds of names are written here — some of them famous, but most of them obscure, and all destined at no very distant day to perish where they stand. On the chimney-piece at the right of the fire-place, which is named the "Actors' Pillar," many actors have inscribed their signatures. Edmund Kean wrote his name here — probably the greatest Shakespearean actor that ever lived — and with what soulful veneration and spiritual sympathy it is awful even to try to imagine. Sir Walter Scott's name is scratched with a diamond on the window — "W. Scott." That of Thackeray appears on the ceiling, and close by it is that of Helen Faucit. Vestris is written near the fire-place. Mark Lemon and Charles Dickens are together on the opposite wall. The catalogue would be endless ; and it is not of these offerings of fealty that you think when you sit and muse alone in that mysterious chamber. As once again I conjure up that strange and solemn scene, the sunshine rests in checkered squares upon the ancient floor, the motes swim in the sunbeams, the air is very cold, the place is hushed as death, and over it all there broods an atmosphere of grave suspense

and hopeless desolation — a sense of
dous energy stricken dumb and frozen into silence,
and past and gone forever.

The other rooms which are shown in the Shakespeare cottage possess but few points of special interest. Opposite to the birth-chamber, at the rear, there is a small apartment, in which is displayed "the Stratford Portrait" of the poet. This painting is supposed to have been owned by the Clopton family, and to have fallen into the hands of William Hunt, an old resident of Stratford, who bought their mansion of the Cloptons, in 1758. The adventures through which it passed can only be conjectured. It does not appear to have been valued, and although it remained in the house, it was cast away amongst lumber and rubbish. In process of time it was painted over and changed into a different subject. Then it fell a prey to dirt and damp. There is a story that the little boys of the tribe of Hunt were accustomed to use it as a target for their arrows. At last, after the lapse of a century, the grandson of William Hunt showed it by chance to an expert artist, who luckily surmised that a valuable portrait might perhaps exist beneath its muddy surface. It was carefully cleaned. A thick beard and a pair of mustaches were removed, and the face of Shakespeare emerged upon the canvas. It is not pretended that this portrait was painted in Shakespeare's time. The very close resemblance which it bears, in attitude, dress colours, and other peculiarities, to the painted bust of the poet in Stratford church seems clearly to indicate that it was a modern copy of that work. Upon a brass plate affixed to it is the following inscription: "This portrait of Shakespeare, after being in the possession of Mr. William Oakes Hunt, town-clerk of Stratford, and his family, for upward of a century, was restored to its original condition by Mr. Simon Collins of London, and, being considered a portrait of much interest and value, was given by Mr. Hunt to the town of Stratford-upon-Avon, to be preserved in Shakespeare's house, 23d April, 1862." There, accordingly, it remains, and in memory's association with the several other dubious presentments of the poet, cheerfully adds to the mental confusion of the pilgrim who would fain form an accurate ideal of Shakespeare's appearance. Standing in its presence, it was worth while to reflect that there are only two authentic representations of Shakespeare in existence — the Droeshout portrait and the Gerard Johnson bust. They may not be perfect works of art; they may not do perfect justice to the original; but they were seen and accepted by persons to whom Shakespeare had been a living companion. The bust was sanctioned by his children; the portrait — fourteen times copied and engraved within fifty years after his death — was sanctioned by his friend Ben Jonson, and by his brother actors Heminge and Condell, who prefixed it, in 1623, to the first folio of his works. Standing amongst the relics

The Home of Shakespeare

which have been gathered into a museum in an apartment on the ground-floor of the cottage. It is essential also to remember how often "the wish is father to the thought" that sanctifies the uncertain memorials of the distant past. Several of the most suggestive documents, though, which bear upon the vague and shadowy record of Shakespeare's life are preserved in this place. Here is a deed, made in 1596, which proves that this house was his father's residence. Here is the only letter addressed to him which is known to exist — the letter of Richard Quiney (1598) asking for the loan of thirty pounds. Here is his declaration in a suit, in 1604, to recover the price of some malt that he had sold to Philip Rogers. Here is a deed, dated 1609, on which is the autograph of his brother Gilbert, who represented him at Stratford in his business affairs while he was absent in London, and who, surviving, it is dubiously said, almost till the period of the Restoration, talked, as a very old man, of the poet's impersonation of Adam in "As You Like It." Here likewise is shown a gold seal ring, found not many years ago in a field near Stratford church, on which, delicately engraved, appear the letters W. S., entwined with a true-lover's knot. It may have belonged to Shakespeare. The conjecture is that it did, and that, since on the last of the three sheets which contain his will the word "seal" is stricken out and the word "hand" substituted, he did not seal this document because he had only just then lost this ring. The supposition is, at least, ingenious. It will not harm the visitor to accept it. Nor, as he stands poring over the ancient and decrepit school-desk which has been lodged in this museum, from the grammar school in High street, will it greatly tax his credulity to believe that the " shining morning face " of the boy Shakespeare once looked down upon it in the irksome quest of his " small Latin and less Greek." They call it " Shakespeare's desk." It is very old, and it is certainly known to have been in the school of the Chapel of the Holy Guild, three hundred years ago. There are other relics, more or less indirectly connected with the great name that is here commemorated. The inspection of them all would consume many days; the description of them would occupy many pages. You write your name in the visitors' book at parting, and perhaps stroll forth into the garden of the cottage, which incloses it at the sides and in the rear, and there, beneath the leafy boughs of the English elm, while your footsteps press " the grassy carpet of this plain," behold growing all around you the rosemary, pansies, fennel, columbines, rue, daisies, and violets, which make the imperishable garland on Ophelia's grave, and which are the fragrance of her solemn and lovely memory.

Thousands of times the wonder must have been expressed that, while the world knows so much about Shakespeare's mind, it should know so little about his history. The date of his birth, even, is established by an inference. The   of Stratford church shows that he was   there in 1564, on the 26th of April. It is said to have been customary to baptize infants on the third day after their birth. It is presumed that the custom followed in this instance, and hence it is deduced that   born on April 23d — a date which, making allowance for the difference between the old and new styles of reckoning time, corresponds to our 3d of May. Equally by an inference it is established that the boy was educated in the free grammar school. The school was there; and any boy of the town, who was seven years old and able to read, could get admission to it. Shakespeare's father, chief alderman of Stratford, and then a man of worldly substance, though afterward he became poor, would surely have wished that his children should grow up in knowledge. To the ancient school-house, accordingly, and the adjacent chapel of the guild — which are still extant, on the southeast corner of Chapel and High streets — the pilgrim confidently traces the footsteps of the poet. These buildings are of singular beauty and quaintness. The chapel dates back to about the middle of the thirteenth century. It was a Roman Catholic institution, founded in 1269, under the patronage of the Bishop of Worcester, and committed to the pious custody of the guild of Stratford. A hospital was connected with it in those days, and Robert de Stratford was its first master. New privileges and

confirmation were granted to the guild by Henry the
Fourth, in 1403 and 1429. The grammar school, established on an endowment of lands and tenements
by Thomas Jolyffe, was set up in association with
it in 1482. Toward the end of the reign of Henry
the Seventh, the whole of the chapel, excepting the
chancel, was torn down and rebuilt under the munificent direction of Sir Hugh Clopton, Lord Mayor of
London, and Stratford's chief citizen and benefactor.
Under Henry the Eighth, when came the stormy
times of the Reformation, the priests were driven out,
the guild was dissolved, and the chapel was despoiled.
Edward the Sixth, however, granted a new charter
to this ancient institution, and with especial precautions reinstated the school. The chapel itself was
used as a school-room when Shakespeare was a
boy, and till as late as the year 1595; and in case
the lad did really go thither (in 1571) as a pupil,
he must have been from childhood familiar with
what is still visible upon its walls — the very remarkable series of grotesque paintings which there
present, as in a pictorial panorama, the history of
the Holy Cross, from its origin as a tree at the
beginning of the world, to its exaltation at Jerusalem. These paintings were brought to light in 1804
in the course of a general repairing of the chapel,
which then occurred, when the walls were relieved
of thick coatings of whitewash, laid on them long before, in Puritan times, either to spoil or to hide from
the spoiler. This chapel and its contents, in any

case, constitute one of the few remaining spectacles
at Stratford that bring us face to face with Shakespeare. During the last three years of his life he
dwelt almost continually in his house of New Place,
on the corner immediately opposite to this church.
The   of the excavated foundations of
that house indicates what would now be called a
               in its southern front. There,
          was Shakespeare's study; and through
    casement, many and many a time, in storm and
in sunshine, by night and by day, he must have
looked out upon the grim, square tower, the embat-
tled stone wall, and the four tall Gothic windows of
that dark, mysterious temple. The moment your
gaze falls upon it, the low-breathed, horror-stricken
words of Lady Macbeth spring involuntarily to your
lips: —

"The raven himself is hoarse
That croaks the fatal entrance of Duncan
Under my battlements."

New Place, Shakespeare's home at the time of
his death, and presumably the house in which he
died, stood on the northeast corner of High Street
and Chapel Street. Nothing now remains of it but
a portion of its foundations — long buried in the
earth, but found and exhumed in comparatively
recent days. Its gardens have been redeemed,
through the zealous and devoted exertions of Mr.
Halliwell, and have been restored to what is
thought to have been almost their exact condition

when Shakespeare owned them. The crumbling fragments of the foundation are covered with frames of wood and glass. A mulberry-tree — the grandson of the famous mulberry which Shakespeare himself is known to have planted — is growing on the spot once occupied by its renowned ancestor. There is no drawing or print in existence which shows New Place as it was when Shakespeare left it, but there is a sketch of it as it appeared in 1740. The house was made of brick and timber, and was built by Sir Hugh Clopton nearly a century before it became by purchase the property of the poet. Shakespeare bought it in 1597, and in it passed, intermittently, a considerable part of the last nineteen years of his life. It had borne the name of New Place before it came into his possession. The Clopton family parted with it in 1563, and it was subsequently owned by the families of Bott and of Underhill. At Shakespeare's death it was inherited by his eldest daughter, Susanna, wife to Dr. John Hall. In 1643, Mrs. Hall, then seven years a widow, being still its owner and occupant, Henrietta Maria, queen to Charles the First, who had come to Stratford with a part of the royal army, resided for three weeks at New Place, which, therefore, must even then have been the most considerable private residence in the town. Mrs. Hall dying in 1649, aged sixty-six, left it to her only child, Elizabeth, then Mrs. Thomas Nashe, who afterward became Lady

Barnard, wife to Sir Thomas Barnard, and in whom the direct line of Shakespeare ended. After her death the estate was purchased by Sir Edward Walker, in 1675, who ultimately left it to his daughter's husband, Sir John Clopton, and so it once more passed into the hands of the family of its founder. A second Sir Hugh Clopton owned it at the middle of the last century, and under his direction it was repaired, freshly decorated, and furnished with a new front. That proved the beginning of the end of this old structure, as a relic of Shakespeare: for this owner, dying in 1751, bequeathed it to his son-in-law, Henry Talbot, who in 1753 sold it to the most universally execrated iconoclast of modern times, the Rev. Francis Gastrell, vicar of Frodsham, in Cheshire, by whom it was destroyed. Mr. Gastrell, it appears, was a man of large fortune and of equal insensibility. He knew little of Shakespeare, but he knew that the frequent incursion, into his garden, of strangers who came to sit beneath " Shakespeare's mulberry " was a troublesome annoyance. He struck, therefore, at the root of the vexation, and cut down the tree. This was in 1756. The wood was purchased by Thomas Sharp, a watchmaker of Stratford, who subsequently made the solemn declaration that he carried it to his home and converted it into toys and kindred memorial relics. The villagers of Stratford, meantime, incensed at the barbarity of Mr. Gastrell, took their revenge by breaking his windows. In this and in other ways the clergyman was probably made to realize his local unpopularity. It had been his custom to reside during a part of each year in Lichfield, leaving some of his servants in charge of New Place. The overseers of Stratford, having lawful authority to levy a tax, for the maintenance of the poor, on every house in the town valued at more than forty shillings a year, did not, it may be presumed, neglect to make a vigourous use of their privilege, in the case of Mr. Gastrell. The result of their exactions in the sacred cause of charity was at least significant. In 1757 Mr. Gastrell declared that that house should never be taxed again, pulled down the building, sold the materials of which it had consisted, and left Stratford forever. A modern house now stands on a part of the site of what was once Shakespeare's home, and here has been established another museum of Shakespearean relics. None of these relics is of imposing authenticity or of remarkable interest. Among them is a stone mullion, dug up on the site, which must have belonged to a window of the original mansion. This entire estate, bought from different owners, and restored to its Shakespearean condition, became in 1875 the property of the corporation of Stratford. The tract of land is not large. The visitor may traverse the whole of it in a few minutes, although if he obey his inclination he will linger there for hours. The inclosure is about three hundred feet

The Home of   .

ibly   in
The li   of the
from the two   of
is traced in   turf.   is
flourishing, and wears its   a con-
. Other
        and the voluptuous
       in profuse richness, load the air
                    Eastward, at a little dis-
  flows   on. Not far away rises the
    ful spire of the Holy Trinity. A few rooks,
       in the air, and wisely   on some face-
ti   f, send down   the silvery haze
of the summer morning th   yet melancholy caw. The windows of   chapel across
the street twinkle, and keep   ir solemn
On this spot was first waved the mystic wand of
Prospero. Here Ariel sang of dead men's bones
turned into pearl and coral in the deep caverns
of the sea. Here arose into everlasting life Hermione, "as tender as infancy and grace." Here
were created Miranda and Perdita twins of heaven's
own radiant goodness —

"Daffodils
That come before the swallow dares, and take
The winds of March with beauty; violets dim,
But sweeter than the lids of Juno's eyes
Or Cytherea's breath."

To endeavour to touch upon the larger and more
august aspect of Shakespeare's life — when, as his

wonderful sonnets betray, his great heart had felt the devastating blast of cruel passions, and the deepest knowledge of the good and evil of the universe had been borne in upon his soul — would be impious presumption. Happily, to the stroller in Stratford every association connected with him is gentle and tender. His image, as it rises there, is of smiling boyhood, or sedate and benignant maturity; always either joyous or serene, never passionate, or turbulent, or dark. The pilgrim thinks of him as a happy child at his father's fireside ; as a wondering school-boy in the quiet, venerable close of the old Guild Chapel, where still the only sound that breaks the silence is the chirp of birds or the creaking of the church vane : as a handsome, dauntless youth, sporting by his beloved river or roaming through field and forest many miles about; as the bold, adventurous spirit, bent on frolic and mischief, and not averse to danger, leading, perhaps, the wild lads of his village in their poaching depredations on the park of Charlecote ; as the lover, strolling through the green lanes of Shottery, hand in hand with the darling of his first love, while round them the honeysuckle breathed out its fragrant heart upon the winds of night, and overhead the moonlight, streaming through rifts of elm and poplar, fell on their pathway in showers of shimmering silver; and, last of all, as the illustrious poet, rooted and secure in his massive and shining fame, loved by many, and venerated and

mourned by all, borne slowly th   Stratford
church-yard, while the golden bells   in
sorrow, and the   lime-trees   their
blossoms on his bier, to the place of his
      Through all the scenes i   to this
experience the worshipper of S   genius
may follow him every step of the way. The old
     path across the fields to Shottery remains
unchanged. The wild flowers are blooming along
its margin. The white blossoms of the chestnut
hang over it. The green meadows through which
it winds are thickly sprinkled with the gorgeous
scarlet of the poppy. The hamlet of Shottery is
less than a mile from Stratford, stepping westward
toward the sunset; and there, nestled beneath the
elms and almost embowered in vines and roses,
stands the cottage in which Anne Hathaway was
wooed and won. It is even more antiquated in
appearance than the cottage of Shakespeare, and
more obviously a relic of the distant past. It is
built of wood and plaster, ribbed with massive timbers, crossed and visible all along its front,— and
covered with a thatch roof. It fronts eastward,
presenting its southern end to the road. Under
its eaves, peeping through embrasures cut in the
thatch, are four tiny casements, round which the
ivy twines, and the roses wave softly in the wind
of June. The northern end of the structure is
higher than the southern, and the old building,
originally divided into two tenements, is now di-

vided into three. In front of it is a straggling terrace and a large garden. There is a comfortable air of wildness, yet not of neglect, in all its appointments and surroundings. The place is still the abode of labour and lowliness. Entering its parlour you see a stone floor, a wide fire-place, a broad, hospitable hearth, with cosey chimney-corners, and near this an old wooden settle, much decayed but still serviceable, on which Shakespeare may often have sat, with Anne at his side. The plastered walls of this room here and there reveal traces of an oaken wainscot. The ceiling is low. This evidently was the farm-house of a substantial yeoman in the days of Henry the Eighth. The Hathaways had lived in Shottery for forty years prior to Shakespeare's marriage. The poet, then wholly undistinguished, had just turned eighteen, while his bride was nearly twenty-six, and it is often said now that she acted ill in wedding this boy-lover. They were married in November, 1582, and their first child, Susanna, came in the following May. Anne Hathaway must have been a wonderfully fascinating woman, or Shakespeare would not so have loved her; and she must have loved him dearly—as what woman, indeed, could help it?—or she would not thus have yielded to his passion. There is direct testimony to the beauty of his person; and in the light afforded by his writings it requires no extraordinary penetration to conjecture that his brilliant mind, sparkling

The Home of Shakespeare

humour, tender fancy, and impetuous spirit must have made him, in his youth, the very paragon of enchanters. It is not known where they lived during the first years after their marriage. Perhaps in this cottage at Shottery. Perhaps with Hamnet and Judith Sadler, for whom their twins, born in 1585, were named Hamnet and Judith. Her father's house assuredly would have been chosen for Anne's refuge, when presently, in 1586, Shakespeare was obliged to leave his wife and children, and go away to London to seek his fortune. He did not buy New Place till 1597, but it is known that in the meantime he came to his native country once every year. It was in Stratford that his son Hamnet died, in 1596. Anne and her children probably had never left the town. They show her bedstead and other bits of her furniture, together with certain homespun sheets of everlasting linen, that are kept as heirlooms to this day, in the garret of the Shottery cottage. Here is the room that must often have welcomed the poet when he came home from his labours in the great city. It is a very homely and humble place, but the sight of it makes the heart thrill with a strange and incommunicable awe. You cannot wish to speak when you are standing there. You are scarcely conscious of the low rustling of the leaves outside, the far off sleepy murmuring of the brook, or the faint fragrance of woodbine and maiden's-blush that is wafted in at the open casement, and that swathes in nature's incense a memory sweeter than itself.

Associations may be established by fable as well as by fact. There is but little reason to believe the old legendary tale, first recorded by Rowe, that Shakespeare, having robbed the deer park of Sir Thomas Lucy, of Charlecote, was so severely prosecuted by that magistrate that he was compelled to quit Stratford and shelter himself in London. Yet the story has twisted itself into all the lives of Shakespeare, and whether received or rejected, has clung till this day to the house of Charlecote. That noble mansion — a genuine specimen, despite a few modern alterations, of the architecture of Queen Elizabeth's time — is found on the western bank of the Avon, about three miles southwest from Stratford. It is a long, rambling, three-storied palace — quite as finely quaint as old St. James's in London, and not altogether unlike that edifice in general character — with octagon turrets, gables, balustrades, Tudor casements, and great stacks of chimneys, so densely closed in by elms of giant growth that you can scarce distinguish it through the foliage till you are close upon it. It was erected in 1558 by Thomas Lucy, who in 1578 was sheriff of Warwickshire, and who was knighted by Queen Elizabeth in 1593. There is a silly, wretched old ballad in existence, attributed to Shakespeare, which, it is said, was found affixed to Lucy's park gate, and gave him great offense.

He must have been more than only sensitive to he could really have been annoyed by manifestly scurrilous ebullition of the and the blockhead supposing, indeed, ever saw it. In it he is called a "knight," he did not become until at least five years after the time when this precious document is alleged to have been written. The writing, proffered as the work of Shakespeare, is undoubtedly a forgery. There is but one existing reason to think that the poet ever cherished a grudge against the Lucy family, and that is the coarse allusion to the name which is found in the "Merry Wives of Windsor." There was, apparently, a second Sir Thomas Lucy, later than the sheriff, who was still more of the Puritanic breed, while Shakespeare, evidently, was a Cavalier. It is possible that in a youthful frolic the poet may have poached on Sheriff Lucy's preserves. Even so, the affair was extremely trivial. It is possible, too, that in after years he may have had reason to dislike the extra-Puritanical neighbour. Some memory of the tradition will, of course, haunt the traveller's thoughts as he strolls by Hatton Rock and through the antiquated villages of Hampton and Charlecote, and up the broad leafy avenue to Charlecote House. But this discordant recollection is soon smoothed away by the peaceful loveliness of the ramble — past aged hawthorns that Shakespeare himself must have seen, and under the boughs of beeches, limes, and drooping willows, where every footstep falls on wild flowers, or on a cool green turf that is softer than Indian silk and as firm and springy as the sands of the sea-beaten shore. Thought of Sir Thomas Lucy will not be otherwise than kind, neither, when the stranger in Charlecote church reads the epitaph with which the old knight himself commemorated his wife: "All the time of her life a true and faithful servant of her good God; never detected of any crime or vice; in religion most sound; in love to her husband most faithful and true; in friendship most constant; to what in trust was committed to her most secret; in wisdom excelling; in governing her house and bringing up of youth in the fear of God that did converse with her most rare and singular. A great maintainer of hospitality; greatly esteemed of her betters; misliked of none, unless of the envious. When all is spoken that can be said, a woman so furnished and garnished with virtue as not to be bettered, and hardly to be equalled of any. As she lived most virtuously, so she died most godly. Set down by him that best did know what hath been written to be true, Thomas Lucy." A narrow formalist he may have been, and a severe magistrate in his dealings with scapegrace youths, and perhaps a haughty and disagreeable neighbour; but there is a touch of genuine manhood, high feeling, and virtuous and self-respecting character in these lines which instantly wins the response of sympathy. If Shakespeare really shot the deer of Thomas Lucy, the injured gentleman had a right to feel annoyed. Shakespeare, boy or man, was not a saint, and those who so account him can have read his works to but little purpose. He can bear the full brunt of all his faults. He does not need to be canonized.

This ramble to Charlecote — one of the prettiest walks about Stratford — was, it may surely be supposed, often taken by Shakespeare. He would pass the old mill bridge (new in 1599), which still spans the Avon a little way to the south of the church. The quaint, sleepy mill — clad now with moss and ivy — which adds such a charm to the prospect, was doubtless fresh and bright in those distant days. More lovely to the vision, though, it never could have been than it is at present. The gaze of Shakespeare assuredly dwelt on it with pleasure. His footsteps may be traced, also, in fancy, to the region of the old college building (demolished in 1799), which stood in the southern part of Stratford, and was the home of his friend John Combe, factor of Fulke Greville, Earl of Warwick. Still another of his walks must have tended northward through Welcombe, where he was the owner of lands, to the portly manor of Clopton. On what is called the "Ancient House," which stands on the west side of High Street, not far from New Place, he may often have looked, as he strolled past to the inns of the Boar and the Red Horse. This building, dated 1596, survives, notwithstanding some modern touches of rehabilitation, as a beautiful specimen of Tudor architecture in one at least of its most charming features, the carved and timber-crossed gable. It is a house of three stories, containing parlour, sitting-room, kitchen, and several bedrooms, besides cellars and brew-shed; and when sold at auction, August 23d, 1876, it brought £400. There are other dwellings fully as old in Stratford, but they have been newly painted and otherwise changed. This is a genuine piece of antiquity, and vies with the grammar school of the guild, under whose pent-house the poet could not have failed to pass whenever he went abroad from New Place. Julius Shaw, one of the five witnesses to his will, lived in a house close by the grammar school; and here, it is reasonable to think, Shakespeare would often pause for a chat with his friend and neighbour. In all the little streets by the river-side, which are ancient and redolent of the past, his image seems steadily familiar. In Dead Lane (now called Chapel Lane) he owned a little, low cottage, bought of Walter Getley in 1602, and only destroyed within the present century. These and kindred shreds of fact, suggesting the poet as a living man, and connecting him, howsoever vaguely, with our human, every-day experience, are seized on with peculiar zest by the pilgrim in Stratford. Such a votary, for example, never doubts that Shakespeare was a frequenter, in leisure and convivial hours, of the ancient Red Horse Inn. It stood there in his day as it stands now, on the right-hand side of Bridge street, westward from the Avon. There are many other taverns in the town — the Shakespeare, the Falcon, the White Hart, the Rose and Crown, the old Red Lion, and the Cross Keys being a few of them — but the Red Horse takes precedence of all its kindred, in the fascinating, because suggestive, attribute of antiquity. Moreover, it was the Red Horse that harboured Washington Irving, the pioneer of American worshippers at the shrine of Shakespeare; and the American explorer of Stratford would cruelly sacrifice his peace of mind if he were to repose under any other roof. The Red Horse is a rambling, three-story building, entered through a large archway, which leads into a long, straggling yard, adjacent to many offices and stables. On one side of the hall of entrance is found the smoking-room and bar; on the other are the coffee-room and several sitting-rooms. Above are the chambers. It is a thoroughly old-fashioned inn — such a one as we may suppose the Boar's Head to have been, in the time of Prince Henry; such a one as untravelled Americans only know in the pages of Dickens. The rooms are furnished in plain and homely style, but their associations readily deck them with the fragrant garlands of memory. When Drayton and Jonson came down to visit "gentle Will" at Stratford, they could scarcely have omitted to quaff the glorious ale of Warwickshire in this cosey parlour.

When Queen Henrietta Maria was ensconced at New Place, the honoured guest of Shakespeare's elder and favourite daughter, the general of the royal forces quartered himself at the Red Horse, and then doubtless there was enough and to spare of merry revelry within its walls. A little later the old house was soundly peppered by the Roundhead bullets, and the whole town was overrun with the close-cropped, psalm-singing soldiers of the Commonwealth. In 1742 Garrick and Macklin lodged in the Red Horse, and hither again came Garrick in 1769, to direct the great Shakespeare Jubilee, which was then most dismally accomplished, but which is always remembered to the great actor's credit and honour. Betterton, no doubt, lodged here when he came to Stratford in quest of reminiscences of Shakespeare. The visit of Irving, supplemented with his delicious chronicle, has led to what might be called almost the consecration of the parlour in which he sat and the chamber in which he slept. They still keep the poker — now marked "Geoffrey Crayon's sceptre" — with which, as he sat there in long, silent, and ecstatic meditation, he so ruthlessly prodded the fire in the narrow, tiny grate. They keep also the chair in which he sat — a plain, straight-backed arm-chair, with a hair-cloth seat, much worn in these latter days by the incumbent devotions of the faithful, but duly marked, on a brass label, with his renowned and treasured name. Thus genius can sanctify even the humblest objects,

To pass rapidly in review the little that is known of Shakespeare's life is, nevertheless, to be impressed not by its incessant and amazing literary but by quick succession of its salient The vitality must have been enormous that created in so short a time such a number and variety of works of the first class. The same "quick spirit" would naturally have kept in agitation all the elements of his daily experience. Descended from an ancestor who had fought for the Red Rose on Bosworth Field, he was born to repute as well as competence, and during his early childhood he received instruction and training in a comfortable home. He escaped the plague, which was raging in Stratford when he was an infant, and which took many victims. He went to school when seven years old, and left it when about fourteen. He then had to work for his living — his once opulent father having fallen into misfortune — and he became an apprentice to a butcher, or else a lawyer's clerk (there were seven lawyers in Stratford at that time), or else a school-teacher. Perhaps he was all three — and more. It is conjectured that he saw the players who from time to time acted in the Guildhall, under the auspices of the corporation of Stratford; that he attended the religious entertainments which were customarily given in the neighbouring city of Coventry; and that in particular he witnessed the elaborate and sumptuous pageants with which in 1575 the Earl of Leicester welcomed Queen Elizabeth to Kenilworth Castle. He married at eighteen; and, leaving a wife and three children in Stratford, he went up to London at twenty-two. His entrance into theatrical life immediately followed — in what capacity it is impossible to judge. One dubious account says that he held horses for the public at the theatre door; another that he got employment as a prompter to the actors. It is certain that he had not been in the theatrical business long before he began to make himself felt. At twenty-eight he was known as a prosperous author. At twenty-nine he had acted with Burbage before Queen Elizabeth; and while Spenser had extolled him in the "Tears of the Muses," the envious Green had disparaged him in the "Groat's-worth of Wit." At thirty-three he had acquired wealth enough to purchase New Place, the principal residence in his native town, where now he placed his family and established his home, — himself remaining in London, but visiting Stratford at frequent intervals. At thirty-four he was heard of as the actor of Knowell in Ben Jonson's comedy, then new, of "Every Man in his Humour," and he received the glowing encomium of Meres in "Wit's Treasury." At thirty-eight he had written "Hamlet" and "As You Like It," and, moreover, he was now become the owner of more estate in Stratford, costing him £320. At forty-one he made his largest purchase, buying for £440 the tithes of Stratford, Old Stratford, Bishopton, and Welcombe. In the mean time he had smoothed the declining years of his father, and had followed him with love and duty to the grave. Other domestic bereavements likewise befell him, and other worldly cares and duties were laid upon his hands, but neither grief nor business could check the fertility of his brain. Within the next ten years he wrote, among other great plays, "Othello," "Lear," "Macbeth," and "Coriolanus." At about forty-eight he seems to have disposed of his shares in the two London theatres with which he had been connected, the Blackfriars and the Globe, and shortly afterward, his work as we possess it being well-nigh completed, he retired finally to his Stratford home. That he was the comrade of all the bright spirits who glittered in "the spacious times" of Elizabeth, many of them have left their personal testimony. That he was the king of them all, is evidenced in his works. The Sonnets seem to disclose that there was a mysterious, almost a tragical, passage in his life, and that he was called to bear the secret burden of a great and perhaps a calamitous personal grief — one of those griefs, too, which, being germinated by sin, are endless in the punishment they entail. Happily, however, no antiquarian student of Shakespeare's time has yet succeeded in coming very near to the man. While he was in London he used to frequent the

Falcon Tavern and the Mermaid, and he lived at one time in Bishopsgate street, and at another time in Clink street, in Southwark. As an actor his name has been associated with his own characters of Adam, Friar Lawrence, and the Ghost of King Hamlet, and a contemporary reference declared him "excellent in the quality he professes." Many of his manuscripts, it is probable, perished in the fire which consumed the Globe Theatre, in 1613. He passed his last days in his home at Stratford, and died there, somewhat suddenly, on his fifty-second birth-day. This event, it may be worth while to observe, occurred within thirty-three years of the execution of Charles the First, under the Puritan Commonwealth of Oliver Cromwell. The Puritan spirit, intolerant of the play-house and of all its works, must even then have been gaining formidable strength. His daughter Judith, aged thirty-two at the time of his death, survived him forty-six years, and the whisper of tradition says that she was a Puritan. If so, the strange and seemingly unaccountable disappearance of whatever play-house papers he may have left behind him at Stratford should not be obscure. The suggestion is likely to have been made before; and also it is likely to have been supplemented with a reference to the great fire in London in 1666 — (which in consuming St. Paul's Cathedral burned an immense quantity of books and manuscripts that had been brought from all the threatened parts of the city and

The Home of Shakespeare

heaped beneath its arches for safety) — as probably the final and effectual holocaust of almost piece of print or writing that might have served to the history of Shakespeare. In his per- no less than in the fathomless resources of his he baffles all scrutiny, and stands forever alone.

> "Others abide our question; thou are free:
> We ask, and ask; thou smilest and art still —
> Out-topping knowledge."

It is impossible to convey in words even an adequate suggestion of the prodigious and overwhelming sense of peace that falls upon the soul of the pilgrim in Stratford church. All the cares and struggles and trials of mortal life, all its failures, and equally all its achievements, seem there to pass utterly out of remembrance. It is not now an idle reflection that "the paths of glory lead but to the grave." No power of human thought ever rose higher or went further than the thought of Shakespeare. No human being, using the weapons of intellectual achievement, ever accomplished so much. Yet here he lies — who was once so great! And here also, gathered around him in death, lie his parents, his children, his descendants, and his friends. For him and for them the struggle has long since ended. Let no man fear to tread the dark pathway that Shakespeare has trodden before him. Let no man, standing at this grave, and seeing and feeling that all the vast labours of that celestial genius end here at last in a handful of dust, fret and grieve any more over the puny and evanescent toils of to-day, so soon to be buried in oblivion! In the simple performance of duty, and in the life of the affections, there may be permanence and solace. The rest is an "unsubstantial pageant." It breaks, it changes, it dies, it passes away, it is forgotten; and though a great name be now and then for a little while remembered, what can the remembrance of mankind signify to him who once wore it? Shakespeare, there is good reason to believe, set precisely the right value alike upon renown in his own time and the homage of posterity. Though he went forth, as the stormy impulses of his nature drove him, into the great world of London, and there laid the firm hand of conquest upon the spoils of wealth and power, he came back at last to the peaceful home of his childhood; he strove to garner up the comforts and everlasting treasures of love at his own hearth-stone; he sought an enduring monument in the hearts of friends and companions; and so he won for his stately sepulchre the garland not alone of glory, but of affection. Through the tall eastern window of the chancel of Holy Trinity Church the morning sunshine, broken into many-coloured light, streams in upon the grave of Shakespeare, and gilds his bust upon the wall above it. He lies close by the altar, and every circumstance of his place of burial is eloquent of his hold upon the affectionate esteem of his contemporaries, equally as a man, a Christian, and a famous poet. The line of graves beginning at the north wall of the chancel, and extending across to the south, seems devoted entirely to Shakespeare and his family, with but one exception. The pavement that covers them is of that bluish-gray slate or freestone which in England is sometimes called black marble. Beneath it there are vaults which may have been constructed by the monks when this church was built, far back in the eleventh or twelfth century. In the first of these, under the north wall, rests Shakespeare's wife. The next is that of the poet himself, bearing the world-famed words of blessing and imprecation. Then comes the grave of Thomas Nashe, husband to Elizabeth Hall, the poet's granddaughter. Next is that of Dr. John Hall, husband to his daughter Susanna, and close beside him rests Susanna herself. The grave-stones are laid east and west, and all but one present inscriptions. That one is under the south wall, and, possibly, covers the dust of Judith Thomas Quiney—the youngest daughter of Shakespeare, who, surviving her three children, and thus leaving no descendants, died in 1662. Upon the gravestone of Susanna an inscription has been intruded commemorative of Richard Watts, who is not, however, known to have had any relationship with either Shakespeare or his descendants. The remains of many other persons may perhaps be entombed in these vaults. Shakespeare's father, who died in 1661, and his mother, Mary Arden, who died in 1608, were buried somewhere in this church. His infant sisters Joan, Margaret, and Anne, and his brother Richard, who died, aged thirty-nine, in 1613, may also have been laid to rest in this place. Of the death and burial of his brother Gilbert there is no record. His sister Joan, the second — Mrs. Hart — would naturally have been placed with her relatives. His brother Edmund, dying in 1607, aged twenty-seven, is under the pavement of St. Saviour's Church in Southwark. The boy Hamnet, dying before his father had risen into much local eminence, rests, probably, in an undistinguished grave in the church-yard. The family of Shakespeare seems to have been short-lived, and it was soon extinguished. He himself died at fifty-two. Judith's children all perished young. Susanna bore but one child — Elizabeth — who, as already mentioned, became successively Mrs. Nashe and Lady Barnard, and she, dying in 1670, was buried at Abington. She left no children by either husband, and in her the race of Shakespeare became extinct. That of Anne Hathaway also has nearly disappeared, the last living descendant of the Hathaways being Mrs. Taylor, the present occupant of Anne's cottage at Shottery. Thus, one by one, from the pleasant gardened town of Stratford, they went to take up their long abode in that old church, which was ancient even in their infancy, and which, watching through the centuries in its monastic solitude on the shore of Avon, has seen their lands and houses devastated by flood and fire, the places that knew them changed by the tooth of time, and almost all the associations of their lives obliterated by the improving hand of destruction.

One of the oldest and most interesting Shakespearean documents in existence is the narrative, by a traveller named Dowdall, of his observations in Warwickshire, and of his visit on April 10, 1693, to Stratford church. He describes therein the bust and the tomb-stone of Shakespeare, and he adds these remarkable words: " The clerk that showed me this church is above eighty years old. He says that not one, for fear of the curse above said, dare touch his grave-stone, though his wife and daughter did earnestly desire to be laid in the same grave with him." Writers in modern days have been pleased to disparage that inscription, and to conjecture that it was the work of a sexton, and not of the poet; but no one denies that it has accomplished its purpose in preserving the sanctity of Shakespeare's rest. Its rugged strength, its simple pathos, its fitness, and its sincerity make it felt as unquestionably the utterance of Shakespeare himself, when it is read upon the slab that covers him. There the musing traveller full well conceives how dearly the poet must have loved the beautiful scenes of his birth-place, and with what intense longing he must have desired to sleep undisturbed in the most sacred spot in their bosom. He doubtless had some premonition of his approaching death. Three months before it came he drafted his will. A little later he attended to the marriage of his younger daughter. Within less than a month of his death he executed the will, and thus set his affairs in perfect order. His handwriting in the three signatures to that paper conspicuously exhibits the uncertainty and lassitude of shattered nerves. He was probably quite worn out. Within the space, at the utmost, of twenty-five years, he had written his thirty-seven plays, his one hundred and fifty-four sonnets, and his two or more long poems; had passed through much and painful toil and through many sorrows; had made his fortune as author, actor, and manager; and had superintended, to excellent advantage, his property in London and his large estates in Stratford and its neighbourhood. The proclamation of health with which the will begins was doubtless a formality of legal custom. The story that he died of drinking too hard at a merry meeting with Drayton and Ben Jonson is the merest hearsay and gossip. If in those last days of fatigue and presentiment he wrote the epitaph that has ever since marked his grave, it would naturally have taken the plainest fashion of speech. Such, at all events, is its character; and no pilgrim to the poet's shrine could wish to see it changed:—

The Home of Shakespeare.

" Good frend for Iesvs sake forbeare,
To digg the dvst encloased heare :
Blese be ye man yt spares thes stones
And cvrst be he yt moves my bones."

It was once surmised that the poet's solicitude lest his bones might be disturbed in death grew out of his intention to take with him into the grave a confession that the works which now "follow him" were written by another hand. Persons have been found who actually believe that a man who was great enough to write "Hamlet" could be little enough to feel ashamed of it, and, accordingly, that Shakespeare was only hired to play at authorship as a screen for the actual author. It might not, perhaps, be strange that a desire for singularity, which is one of the worst literary fashions of this capricious age, should prompt to the rejection of the conclusive and overwhelming testimony to Shakespeare's genius which has been left by Shakespeare's contemporaries, and which shines out in all that is known of his life. It is strange that a doctrine should get itself asserted which is subversive of common reason, and contradictory to every known law of the human mind. This conjectural confession of poetic imposture, of course, has never been exhumed. There came a time in the present century when, as they were making repairs in the chancel pavement of the Holy Trinity (the entire chancel was renovated in 1834), a rift was accidentally made in the Shakespeare vault. Through this, though not without misgiving, the sexton peeped in upon the poet's remains. He saw all that was there, and he saw nothing but a pile of dust.

The antique font from which the infant Shakespeare must have received the sacred water of Christian baptism is still preserved in this church. It was thrown aside and replaced by a new one about the middle of the seventeenth century. Many years afterward it was found in the charnel-house. When that was destroyed, it was cast into the church-yard. In later times the parish clerk used it as a trough to his pump. It passed then through the hands of several successive owners, till at last, in days that had learned to value the past and the associations connected with its illustrious names, it found its way back again to the sanctuary from which it had suffered such a rude expulsion. It is still a beautiful stone, though somewhat soiled and crumbled.

On the north wall of the chancel, above his grave, and near to "the American window," is placed Shakespeare's monument. It is known to have been erected there within seven years after his death. It consists of a half-length effigy, placed beneath a fretted arch, with entablature and pedestal, between two Corinthian columns of black marble, gilded at base and top. Above the entablature appear the armorial bearings of Shakespeare — a pointed spear on a bend sable, and a silver falcon on a tasselled helmet, supporting a spear. Over

this   emblem is a   head, and on each
side of it sits a carven cherub, one holding a spade,
the other an inverted torch. In front of the
is a cushion, upon which both hands rest, holding a
scroll and a pen. Beneath is an inscription in Latin
and English, supposed to have been furnished by
the poet's son-in-law, Dr. Hall. The bust was cut
by Gerard Johnson, a native of Amsterdam, and by
occupation a "tomb-maker." The material is a soft
stone, and the work, when first set up, was painted
in the colours of life. Its peculiarities indicate that
it was copied from a mask of the features taken
after death. Many persons believe that this mask
has since been found, and busts of Shakespeare
have been based upon it, both by W. R. O'Donovan
and William Page. In September, 1746, John Ward,
grandfather of Mrs. Siddons, having come to Stratford with a theatrical company, gave a performance
of "Othello," in the Guildhall, and devoted its proceeds to reparation of the Gerard Johnson effigy,
then somewhat damaged by time. The original
colours were then carefully restored and freshened.
In 1793, under the direction of Malone, this bust,
together with the image of John Combe — a recumbent statue near the eastern wall of the chancel —
was coated with white paint. From that plight it
was extricated a few years ago by the assiduous
skill of Simon Collins, who immersed it in a bath
which took off the white paint and restored the colours. The eyes are painted of a light hazel, the hair

and pointed beard of auburn, the face and hands of flesh-tint. The dress consists of a scarlet doublet with a rolling collar, and closely buttoned down the front, worn under a loose black gown without sleeves. The upper part of the cushion is green, the lower part crimson, and this object is ornamented with gilt tassels. The stone pen that used to be in the right hand of the bust was taken from it toward the end of the last century by a young Oxford student, and being dropped by him upon the pavement, was broken. A quill pen has been put in its place. This is the inscription beneath the bust : —

>Ivdicio Pylivm, genio Socratem, arte Maronem,
>Terra tegit, popvlvs mæret, Olympvs habet.

Stay, passenger, why goest thov by so fast?
Read, if thov canst, whom enviovs Death hath plast
Within this monvment : SHAKSPEARE : with whome
Qvick Natvre dide ; whose name doth deck ye tombe
Far more than cost ; sieth all y^t he hath writt
Leaves living art bvt page to serve his witt.

>Obiit Ano. Doi. 1616. Ætatis 53. Die. 23. Ap.

The erection of the old castles, cathedrals, monasteries, and churches of England must, of course, have been accomplished, little by little, in laborious exertion protracted through many years. Stratford church, probably more than seven centuries old, presents a mixture of architectural styles, in which Saxon simplicity and Norman grace are beautifully mingled. Different parts of the structure were, doubtless, built at different times. It is fashioned in the customary crucial form, with a square tower, a six-sided spire, and a fretted battlement all around its roof. Its windows are Gothic. The approach to it is across an old church-yard thickly sown with graves, through a lovely green avenue of blossoming lime-trees, leading to a carven porch on its north side. This avenue of foliage is said to be the copy of one that existed there in Shakespeare's day, through which he must often have walked, and through which at last he was carried to his grave. Time itself has fallen asleep in this ancient place. The low sob of the organ only deepens the awful sense of its silence and its dreamless repose. Beeches, yews, and elms grow in the church-yard, and many a low tomb and many a leaning stone are there in the shadow, gray with moss and mouldering with age. Birds have built their nests in many crevices in the time-worn tower, round which at sunset you may see them circle, with chirp of greeting or with call of anxious discontent. Near by flows the peaceful river, reflecting the grey spire in its dark, silent, shining waters. In the long and lonesome meadows beyond it the primroses stand in their golden banks among the clover, and the frilled and fluted bell of the cowslip, hiding its single drop of blood in its bosom, closes its petals as the night comes down.

Northward, at a little distance from the Church

of the Holy Trinity, stands, on the west bank of the Avon, the building which will henceforth be famous through the world as the Shakespeare Memorial. Its dedication, assigned for the 23d of April, 1880, has prompted this glance at the hallowed associations of Stratford. The idea of the Memorial was first suggested in 1864, incidentally to the ceremonies which then commemorated the three-hundredth anniversary of the poet's birth. Ten years later the site for this noble structure was presented to the town by Charles E. Flower, one of its wealthy inhabitants. Contributions of money were then asked, and were liberally given. Americans as well as Englishmen gave large sums. Two years ago, on the 23d of April, the first stone of the Memorial was laid. The structure comprises a theatre, a library, and a picture-gallery. In the theatre the plays of Shakespeare are from time to time to be represented, in a manner as nearly perfect as may be possible. In the library and picture-gallery are to be assembled all the books upon Shakespeare that ever have been published, and all the choice paintings that can be obtained to illustrate his life and his works. As the years pass this will naturally become the principal depository of Shakespearean relics. A dramatic college will grow up in association with the Shakespeare theatre. The spacious gardens which surround the Memorial will augment their loveliness in added expanse of foliage and in greater wealth of floral luxuriance. The mellow tints of age will soften the bright tints of the red brick which mainly composes the building. On its cone-shaped turrets ivy will clamber and moss will nestle. When a few generations have passed, the old town of Stratford will have adopted this now youthful stranger into the race of her venerated antiquities. The same air of poetic mystery which rests now upon his cottage and his grave will diffuse itself around his Memorial; and a remote posterity, looking back to the men and the ideas of to-day, will remember with grateful pride that English-speaking people of the nineteenth century, though they could confer no honour upon the great name of Shakespeare, yet honoured themselves in consecrating this beautiful temple to his memory.

www.ingramcontent.com/pod-product-compliance
Lightning Source LLC
Chambersburg PA
CBHW020245170426
43202CB00008B/233